Is Satan, the devil, a real supernatural being in competition for God's throne, or something of another nature that is suppressed by the church fathers? Much teaching has been based on assumptions of what the word says.

Is Satan, the Devil, a Supernatural Being Fallen from Heaven?

Maston Love Jr., PhD

LifeRich Publishing is a registered trademark of The Reader's Digest Association, Inc.

LifeRich Publishing books may be ordered through booksellers or by contacting:

LifeRich Publishing
1663 Liberty Drive
Bloomington, IN 47403
www.liferichpublishing.com
1 (888) 238-8637

Because of the dynamic nature of the Internet, any web addresses or links contained in this book may have changed since publication and may no longer be valid. The views expressed in this work are solely those of the author and do not necessarily reflect the views of the publisher, and the publisher hereby disclaims any responsibility for them.

Any people depicted in stock imagery provided by Thinkstock are models, and such images are being used for illustrative purposes only. Certain stock imagery © Thinkstock.

Scripture taken from the King James Version of the Bible.

ISBN: 978-1-4897-0896-0 (sc)
ISBN: 978-1-4897-0897-7 (hc)
ISBN: 978-1-4897-0895-3 (e)

Library of Congress Control Number: 2016913194

Print information available on the last page.

LifeRich Publishing rev. date: 8/8/2016

Contents

Preface ix

Is the Devil a Supernatural Being? 1

The Christian's Views of Satan 2

The Jewish View of Satan 2

How the Term *Satan* Originated 3

Greek Concordance 5

Who Is the Devil? 5

The Source of Evil 6

The Doctrine of Demons 7

The Devil of Christendom 9

Modern Beliefs in Devils 10

The Devil of the Bible 11

Bible Devils 12

God and the Devil 13

Sin Personified 14

The Genesis Devil 16

The Serpent in the Garden of Eden 18

Enmity Between the Two Seeds 20

Devils That Tempt 21

Satan and Job 21

Who Hardened Pharaoh's Heart? 23

Who Provoked David to Number Israel? 23

Who Tempted Jesus? 24

Who Was the Devil That Sowed Tares? 26

What Devil Contended with Michael? 26

Are Devils Fallen Angels? 28

Who Was Lucifer? 28

Who Was the Cherub of Ezekiel 28? 30

What Angels "Kept Not Their First Estate"? 31

Jesus Beheld Satan Fall. 32
What Devils Did Jesus Cast Out? 33
Resisting the Devil. 34
God Provides Armor 35
What Do We Fight?. 36
The Future of the Devil 37
The War in Heaven 37
The Devil Bound, Loosed, Destroyed. 39
The Killing of Aaron 40
Jude v. 6. 42
Is This Proof of a Supernatural Devil? 42
Human Beings as Angels 46
What Angels Were Peter and Jude Talking About?. 46
Was the Rebellion in Heaven Before Adam?. 51
When Will Satan Be Cast Out of Heaven? Was He Ever in Heaven? . 52
Taking a Look at Some Symbols 52
When Was Satan Cast Out of Heaven? 53
The Book of Revelation 53
Revelation 12 Tells a Story of Two Wonders that John Saw in Heaven 57
The King of Tyrus 58
Who Is the Prince?. 58
The King of Tyrus 60
The Six Things Listed: Do They Prove the King of Tyrus Was a
    Supernatural Being?. 61
Precious Stones. 62
The Anointed Cherub (Choreb, Kerub: Plural Cherubim) 63
What about Him Being Created?. 66
Whom Did God Send to Kill and Destroy Tyrus and the King? 69
Lucifer's Origin: How Did Lucifer Become Satan?. 70
Where Did the Word Lucifer Come From and What Is Its Meaning?. 71
Why Does the Church Believe Isaiah 14:12 to Be Lucifer, the
    Devil, a Supernatural Being Cast Out of Heaven? 72
Was the Devil Ever in Heaven? 75
Satan as an Angel. 76
Who Was the Satan That Caused Job Such Terror? 78
Job. 78

Is Job's Satan a Supernatural Being?. 79
The Lord's Response. 83
What About the Calamities of Tempest and Disease That Befell Job? 85
Scripture in Which *Satan* Is Untranslated 85
Satan Means Only *Adversary* 87
Was Peter a Satan?. 88
Who Hindered Paul? Was It Satan, Who Was Cast Out of Heaven? . 90
Does This Prove a Supernatural Being? 91
Where Does the Devil Live?. 92
A Few Examples. 92
Satan or the Devil in Us. 93
Who Is the Old Man? Adam or Satan?. 94
What Devil Is James Talking About?. 94
The Devil of the New Testament 95
Who Was This Devil? 96
What Did Christ Accomplish in His Death? 97
What Does All This Mean? 98
What Brought Death Into the World? 99
What Is the Cost of Sin? 99
What Did James Say About This?. 99
When a Person Says He Is Filled with the Spirit, What Is He Saying? 100
How Do You Win This War?. 100
Riches 102
Sin. 102
The Spirit as Male Gender 102
Wisdom as Female Gender. 102
Notice 103
The Nation of Israel as a Young Lady. 103
The Family of Christ: Christian Believers. .103
New State of Mind Developed in the Truth. 104
The Spirit of Disobedience 104
The Heart Is a Deceiver and Can Be Your Devil 106
Who Was the Devil in Matthew 23:13–39? The Religious System . . 107
What About Jesus Being Tempted by the Devil? Does This Not
    Prove a Supernatural Being?. 107
Forty Days of Temptation and Fasting. 107

Why Did Jesus Have to Suffer? 108
What About Taking Jesus to the Pinnacle of the Temple? 108
What About Demons? 110
What Were These Devils? 110
What About Devils Being Cast Out in Matthew 12:22? 112
What About the Swine and Devils Being Cast into Them? 114
Hebrews' View of Satan 115
Satan as Prosecutor 117
Define the Word *Satan* 117
Define the Word *Devil* 117
If Satan the Devil Is Not Real, Explain Satan Cast Out of Heaven
    to Earth as in Revelation 12:9 118
The God of Creation Is One 118
Who Was Going Through Egypt to Kill the Firstborn? 119
If Satan Is Not a Supernatural Being, Why Did Paul Say This? 120
How Do We Fight It? 121
Resource Helps 122
Part Two: Cherubim 123
Cherubim 124
Cherubim 132
What Is the Difference in These Two Cherubim? 133
How Do God and Man Become One? 135
The Cherubim of the Natural Man 138
Why Cannot the Natural Man See the Deep Things of God? 139
What Must Be Changed? 139
Man in God's Image? How? 140
How Do We Know He Has Returned? 141
Where There Is No Ark 143
Circle of Life 144
Ezekiel's Cherubim 144
Hebrew and Greek Words with Definitions 149
Hebrew and Greek Words and Theme Meaning 151
References 152
Test Questions 154
Is Satan a Supernatural Fallen Angel? 157

Preface

In this full gospel study series, it is our intent to provoke students to study and prove their beliefs and convictions. If we are to be "free indeed," it is important to apply ourselves to researching the truth of God's holy Word. To be free, we must know the truth, for that is what sets us free. The full gospel study series is not the full gospel church teaching; it is what we believe to be truth by our research of the subject in scripture.

The truth can be spoken and written. There is no greater truth than he who said, "Jesus said unto him, I am the way, the truth, and life: NO man cometh unto the Father but by me" (John 14:6).

We try to keep with the spirit of the Hebrew words and their meaning. This does not suggest that translations into other languages are not of value, but if we follow the Judean text, we should stay as close to the original as possible. English translations are not the best source.

Over the years, Christianity has trained us to recruit believers by "being saved," but we haven't sufficiently taught people what the Bible says. This book focuses on the problem of self, Satan and the devil within us, rather than a supernatural being causing evil in the land. Our sin causes the problems. This evil begins in our hearts, and the only way to control and destroy the evil (Satan, the devil) is by renewing our minds.

"The mind if fleshly shall die, but if we have the spirit of Christ, we live" (Romans 8:13). There is no mention of a supernatural enemy of which we must rid ourselves—only that all unrighteousness is sin and causes death, which is the last enemy, the devil. The King James Bible, our primary source, is one of the Christian community's most frequently used Bibles, although we also used other versions for research purpose.

Is the Devil a Supernatural Being?

Some people believe that their greatest problem in life is their battle with a supernatural devil. But if the devil is the problem, we should learn as much as we can about him and find out how to defeat him. We should also study the purpose of Christ's work on earth to learn the truth about Christ, what He came to do, and whether He did it.

James 1:18 says, "Of his own will begat he us with THE WORD OF TRUTH, that we should be a kind of first fruits of his Creatures." In Ephesians 5:26, Paul says, "That he might sanctify and cleanse it with the washing of water by the Word." Also, Christ explained to His disciples in John 15:3, "Now ye are clean through the Word which I have spoken unto you." This is how we cleanse ourselves, by the Word.

Speaking to the Jews in John 8:32, Jesus said; "And ye shall know the truth, and the truth shall make you free." By this statement, the word of truth is styled. In Colossians 1:5, Paul says, "For the hope which is laid up for you in heaven, whereof ye heard before in the Word of the Truth of the Gospel this truth is by which men are saved." (See also 1 Corinthians 15:2.)

We find that the truth of the word of the gospel is designed to cleanse and save mankind while addressing the kingdom of God and those things that concern our Lord Jesus the Christ. "Preaching the kingdom of God, and teaching those things which concern the Lord Jesus Christ, with all confidence, no man forbidding him" (Acts 28:31). Acts 8:12 says, "But when they believed Philip preaching the things concerning the kingdom of God, and the name of Jesus Christ, they were baptized, both men and women."

It is important to know and believe what Jesus Christ taught. In Romans 1:16, Paul says, "For I am not ashamed of the Gospel of Christ: for it is the power of God unto salvation to everyone that believeth to the Jew first and also to the Greek." Notice that we must believe the truth concerning Jesus Christ.

The Christian's Views of Satan

The church teaches and believes, from a fundamentalist view, that Satan was one of God's created angels who went astray and persuaded one-third of the host of heaven to fall. The result was that the heavens and earth were changed because of Satan's sin. On top of all this, the angels took wives and had children who became giants in the land.

Their mission was to destroy, kill, and cause sickness in the land, and to seek and destroy as many of God's people as they could. This belief is mostly based on the war depicted in Revelation 12:1, Job 1:6, Isaiah 14, and Ezekiel 28. However, these books do not prove the existence of a supernatural devil. Fundamentalist Christians teach and believe in a real, supernatural, personal devil—or Satan—as an angel cast out of heaven, who is sending people to burn in hell for all eternity. But is this teaching and belief biblical?

The Jewish View of Satan

The Jewish community believes that Christians are blind to the truth. The Jewish people do not look at Satan as an enemy, but as a helper. Their Bible, *Tanakh,* is quite different from the King James Bible. It is interesting to note that the King James Bible was not copied or taken from the Hebrew Bible. The creation of the King James Bible came from the Bishop Bible and the Vulgate. This became the English-speaking people's Bible.

The Jewish understanding of Satan is not the main focus for their relationship with God. They believe Satan is an agent created by God to help us grow stronger and closer to Him. When Jews are being tried by some obstacle or adversary, they look on Satan as a blessing. Difficulties in their path are viewed as experiences to help them move forward, grow, and develop spiritually. Rabbis refer to Satan as the evil inclination that provides passion and desires. The Jews' word for *Satan* is "HA-Satan," and there is no Lucifer in the Hebrew scripture, unlike in the English King James Version. Lucifer is a Satan cast out of heaven called the devil, which is only a bad translation of the Hebrew word.

How the Term Satan Originated

Over the years, the church has done a good job of maintaining a belief in a fallen angel called Satan, or the devil. Many churches have used Satan to place fear into the hearts of people with the hope of saving them. Being saved requires us to believe that the church has the power to rid us of this evil if we will confess, join the church, and do what the church teaches. However, the church fails to teach us that the evil we face is not a devil from heaven. This evil, and adversary, lives and reigns in our hearts.

Satan is a creation of man that originated in ancient astrology. The Egyptian god called Set represented Satum, or Satan. Later the Persians brought this teaching into Christianity. Set became Satan and became viewed as a person. Before this, there was no Satan. Nevertheless, many Christians believe a tradition that the evil in this world is caused by "cast-down angels," and that the devil of the New Testament is also a fallen angel. The devil, Satan, the dragon, and the beast are all terms used by the church as a way of controlling people. To control people the state always uses religion and creates laws as needed for control.

Set was the enemy of life, the deity of the desert, a god to the people of Egypt at the time of Joseph, who was sold into slavery in Egypt.[1] Erman, Adolf, *Life in Ancient Egypt*, page 282. References to the work of: Carus, Paul: *History of the Devil*, Kindle Edition, Evinity Publishing, Inc. 2009. Page15-17

The word *Satan*, meaning "an adversary," is not translated from Hebrew to Greek and English. It doesn't refer to a specific person, as some believe. It is best to use a Hebrew concordance to find the meaning of the word; English is not the best choice.

In *Strong's Concordance,*[2] we find the Hebrew word *Satan* in listings 7853 and 7854. In Hebrew, Satan is an opponent or adversary of good—not an individual person, but anyone who is adversarial.

There is a group that teaches that a fallen angel named Satan came

---

[1] Erman, Adolf, *Life in Ancient Egypt,* page 282. Kindle Edition by Paul Carus , *The History of the Devil* 2009, Page 15-17.

[2] Strong, James, *Strong's Exhaustive Concordance of the Bible.* Hereafter referred to as *Strong's Concordance.*

into the garden of Eden, had sex with Eve, and was the father of Cain. In chapters 2 and 3 of Genesis, God said that Adam and Eve could eat from all the trees of the garden except one—the tree of knowledge of good and evil. All the beasts and trees of the field were good to eat. If fruit represents sex, that would mean that Adam and Eve could have sex with all other trees or beasts of the field, but not the tree of knowledge of good and evil. That is what some people teach. (See Genesis 2:15.) The beast was more subtle than all the beasts of the field, which would include Adam and Eve. If that is the case, why was it forbidden to have sex with the tree in the midst of the garden? At least it would give them an eye-opening experience. That is better than some sermons I hear today.

There is nothing to suggest that the beast or the tree in the midst of the garden was a fallen angel, as such people teach. The problem lies with the *Book of Enoch* and Dante's *Inferno*. The *Book of Enoch*[3] was considered a heretical book and was not added to the King James Bible; however, it is good reading as fiction. The book suggests that Enoch was caught up, by the hair of his head, into heaven and was given the task of teaching the angels of God other duties that would affect things on earth. Dante's *Inferno,*[4] on the other hand, taught that the soul was tortured according to the type of sin that was committed by the individual and what happened when they entered hell.

Here's a list of words from *Strong's Concordance* that relate to Satan and the devil, to help you understand this subject without having to consult a concordance:

> 7853 Satan: attack, accuse, be an adversary, resist (no mention of a personal devil)
> 7854 An opponent, Satan, the archenemy of good: adversary, Satan, withstand

---

[3] Laurence, Richard, *The Book of Enoch*, 1883.
[4] Altemus, Henry, *Dante's Inferno*, circa 1887.

Greek Concordance

Satanas, Satan—devil is also Chaldean for the word *accuser* (no personal devil here).

Satan is only a word: Definition

1. Attack
2. Accuse
3. Adversary
4. An opponent
5. Enemy of good
6. To withstand
7. Satan—Devil
8. Opposition—7855 Greek
9. Accusation—Greek

Satan is not a personality or fallen angel. Nothing is written about a fallen angel. The words describe the person and their attitude, like Peter being Satan and Judas being a devil. To control Satan or the devil, we must learn to control our thoughts. Fallen angels don't defile us. We are defiled by what lives inside us, as we read in Mark 7:20–23: "That which cometh out of the man, that defileth the man. From within, out of the heart of men, proceeds evil thoughts, adulteries, fornications, and murders, thefts, covetousness, wickedness, deceit, lasciviousness, pride, foolishness: ALL these evils things come from within, defile the man."

Who Is the Devil?

Is there a devil, a real being with an individual personality? If so, who created him, and why does an all-powerful God of righteousness and love permit him to exist? Or is the devil a spirit of evil influence, a force that continually inspires evil and devises mischief? (Could such an influence exist without personality?) Exactly who or what is the devil? Is he a supernatural fallen angel?

Many people through the ages have pondered these questions, and many answers have been offered. Some believe that the devil is a hideous-looking horned creature whose cloven hoofs and spiked tail assist him in presiding over the torture of the wicked dead. Others believe him to be some unidentified agent of evil whose chief business is to defame God, attack righteous men, and stir up evil men against God. Others believe him to be a disobedient fallen angel who long ago was cast out of heaven because of his rebellion against God. Still others hold to a rather vague feeling that the devil is a personality or a spirit of evil or a demon, continually opposing God and all that is good.

But we are convinced that none of these views is correct, and that none of them is wholly and solely Bible supported. How does the Bible use the word *devil*? Jesus addressed His apostles, saying, "Have not I chosen you twelve, and one of you is a devil?" (John 6:70). He doesn't say that "one of you is possessed with a devil," but that "one of you is a devil." On another occasion Jesus spoke similarly to Peter: "Get thee behind me, Satan. Thou art an offense unto me" (Matthew 16:23).

The Source of Evil

What, according to the Bible, is the source of evil if it is not the workings of a literal devil? Jesus strikes at the very root of the matter: evil proceeds from the depths of the human heart. The evil thought allowed to conceive and bring forth sin is the defiling agent to mankind. "For from within, out of the heart or mind of men, proceed evil thoughts, adulteries, fornications, murders, thefts, covetousness, wickedness, deceit, lasciviousness, an evil eye, blasphemy, pride, foolishness: all these evil things come from within, and defile the man" (Mark 7:21–23). These are the words of Jesus, and the language is too plain to be mistaken. How can you or I claim to be pure in heart unless we put away all these thirteen evils that Jesus said defile the man? When we have put away these evils, we have killed the only devil that we need ever fear.

James the servant of God was close enough to the source of divine knowledge to have known what he was talking about, and he declared, "Let no man say when he is tempted, I am tempted of God: for God cannot be tempted with evil, neither tempteth He any man; but every man is tempted, when he is drawn away of his own lust, and enticed. Then when lust hath conceived, it bringeth forth sin: and sin, when it is finished bringeth forth death" (James 1:13–15).

The merciful God never tempts any man to evil, and He never

created a devil to lure us away. The writer witnesses that he never once experienced any such influence in his entire life. "Every man is tempted"— no exceptions. "Every man is tempted, when he is drawn away of his own lust, and enticed." This devil is present in every human being.

The man who steals does so because he lusts to possess that which does not belong to him. The liar lies because it is in his interest to suppress the truth. He wants to save his face, to hide his true identity lest the facts about him be disclosed and his reputation suffers. The proud man or woman is proud because self-importance is natural, and he or she does not make the necessary effort to control it.

It is the development of an uncontrollable taste for intoxicating liquor that brings the alcoholic to a state of degradation almost worse than death itself, and not the influence of a personal devil that operates against the man's will. The immoral man is immoral because he lacks self-control. It is easier for him to give way to his base passions than to banish them. Lust conceives and brings forth sin, but in every case the offender himself is the culprit. And the same is true of anger, malice, jealousy, envy, insensitive, and every other sin that defiles.

The Doctrine of Demons

Where did the belief in a devil, such as is accepted by popular theology, originate? The answer is simple: it originated in the imagination of man himself. From more than seven thousand years of human history on this planet have emerged a multitude of ideas, superstitions, and philosophies. Men have thought and dreamed, rationalized and reasoned, feared and imagined. By nature, men crave security and fear harm.

To satisfy his cravings and explain his fears, primitive man early developed polytheistic faiths that included spirits, demons, and devils of every description. He thought of every healthful breeze, every green tree, every solid rock, and every rain-filled cloud as being possessed with a living spirit that blessed him; sometimes he called it "god" and worshipped it. The lightning that shattered his home or set fire to his forest, or the flood that destroyed his crops, or the disease that threatened his life—all were evil spirits, or demons, or devils, spirits to be ameliorated—if possible—or charmed, or driven off.

Firm belief in demons and devils has been current in every society. Among the ancient Assyrians and Babylonians, superstition was rife; the demonic world was so prolific that its inhabitants were divided into classes, or orders, according to the imagined power of each.

From the most ancient times, the spirit world lay very near to the average Chinaman. Good and evil spirits were objects of religious worship or superstitious fear. Egypt had such a vast array of demons and spirits, it is said, that a definition of each was impossible—every object and every being was possessed with some kind of "demon" or "demons."

The Celtic people (early inhabitants of Great Britain) combined beneficent and maleficent dispositions in their demons, which were magical in their behavior and supernatural in their endowments. The influence of such demons, it was thought, could be resisted by enticing them with piety and virtue.

Even the reasoning Greeks tempered their rationalism with superstition, believing that at death the soul of man went to the heavenly Elysium, but the "shade" went to the underworld, where it lived a shadowy, semi-conscious existence. The ghosts of the dead, they believed, tragically sought vengeance on the living. One had to pass their tombs in silence or attract their fury. Illness and insanity were explained as demonic possession.

Aristotle believed that all men have demons that accompany them during the whole period of their mortal existence. The Stoics were firmly convinced of the reality of demons that, having like passions with men, and responding to their desires and fears, superintended and directed their fortunes.

Outstanding in demonology was the faith of the Persian, who thought of the world as controlled by a dual power of good and evil. These opposing forces were engaged in constant warfare until the last millennial cycles of the world, preceding a day of judgment when perfect man shall, by the aid of the heavenly hosts, overcome the power of evil forever. The Persians conceived of these present forces of evil as under the leadership of their creator Ahriman, who brought them forth to wage war against heaven and earth. These demons, equal in activity to the divine forces created by the power of good, were thought of as spirits or bodiless agents who now wandered about at night in the dreaded form of specters.

The Romans regarded the spirits as helpful to mankind if correctly approached and held in honor, but they feared the larvae, a species of ghosts, for they were the souls of wicked men and gathered as aides about the standard of Ahriman and formed the council of hell.

Where, then, is the source of belief in demons or devils? Not in the Bible, but in paganism.

It seems ridiculously inconsistent to suppose that a God of infinite wisdom would stoop to such nonsense as to ask His children to believe in demons or evil spirits. But in the early centuries after the ministry of Christ, the belief crept into the Christian church as it apostatized from the teachings of Jesus. And today nearly all major religious groups hold some form of this belief. Leading commentators all take for granted the existence of demons or a devil.

The Devil of Christendom

In *Hastings Encyclopedia of Religion and Ethics* Vol.4 page 578-579, we read the following:

> The earliest Fathers of the Church acquainted with the angelology and demonology of Scripture and of Jewish apocalyptic literature, all affirm or imply the existence of spirits good and evil. Opposition to Gnostic speculation led earlier writers to insist on the fact that angels and demons were created beings, while some writers refuse to allow to the former any part in the work of creation. The earlier writers more usually identify the "sons of God" with angels. The legend of the fall of the angels, and the person of Satan especially, led later writers to indulge in speculation as to the problem of evil and the relation of evil spirits to God. It would appear that the majority at least of later writers held the view that angels were capable of sinning, being possessed, like men of free will.

The idea of the devil was founded not in the Bible, but in the thinking of such Alexandrian writers as Clement and Origen. And in the second century, Justin Martyr forged the legend (suggested to him by Genesis 6:2) that Satan and his devils were once good angels who had been deposed for having committed carnal sins with the daughters of men. Justin called them *angeli fornicatores*.

John Milton, the blind poet and theologian, in his epic *Paradise Lost*, formed into symbolic poetry the thinking of the Protestant world in the seventeenth century, picturing a war in the high court's of heaven where dwells the Almighty and from which once pure, bright angels were ejected and cast to earth where they have waged a mighty conflict against God and man.

What was the source of this belief? Let us repeat: not the Bible, but paganism. Persians, Romans, Teutonic's, Tibetans, Jains, Japanese, Indians, Moslems, and almost any ancient people you can mention all recognized spirits or powers of evil. But the Bible does not.

Modern Beliefs in Devils

Even today, the Catholic Church, together with many Protestant denominations, believes at least nominally in the existence of a devil. We quote from M.E. Odell "Preparing the Way," by Hawthorn Books New York page 2. "Intelligent beings created by God have only two fundamental choices: They may choose to love God and serve him, or they can turn away from God and aim only at pleasing themselves. In the latter case they cut themselves off from His goodness and love and therefore they become evil. The good, bright glorious angels who deliberately turned away from God became hideous and evil devils, and Lucifer, the light-bearer as he was called, became Satan, the worst of them all."[5]

Other religious people and groups define the devil less literally, as a symbol or representative power of evil, but their beliefs are often confused and inconsistent. For example, they give to a symbolic devil or power of

---

[5] Odell, M. E., "Preparing the Way," *The New Library of Catholic Knowledge.* Hawthorn Books New York 1962 vol. 1. page 2

evil physical, human, or beastly qualities and abilities (i.e., the devil tempts, the devil defiles, the devil lures into sin). How could a spirit, influence, or unembodied personality have any of these abilities?

The belief in a supernatural devil is rather common among many Christians today. The only problem is that Satan is the problem that causes all their sins and bad habits, but in the end this Satan does not show up to take his part of the punishment. The individuals are to stand and defend themselves before their God. We could remove all these concerns by accepting the fact that sin is not caused by a devil, but by people themselves. A supernatural devil is not supported by any Bible that I know of, or by any scripture that I can find. Our lives can be very fruitful if only we accept the truth and confess that the sin problem in embedded in our hearts, where we need to start making life's adjustments. The supernatural devil doctrine has been encouraged by preachers all over the world, and used to their advantage and for their selfish purpose. It is all about control.

The Devil of the Bible

The words *Satan* and *devil*, as used in the languages in which God spoke to men, have no such ideas as are attached to them by theology. *The Interpreters Dictionary of the Bible,* Abingdon [6]Press 1962 Vol.1 Page 838, vol.4 page 224-228 defines Satan as "the archfiend; chief of the devils; instigator of all evil; the rival of God; the Antichrist," and comments as follows:

> The Hebrew root, from which the name Satan derives, means primarily "obstruct, and oppose." It is used in the Old Testament of obstructing a man's path (Numbers 22:22–23), opposing in war (1 Samuel 29:4), preferring charges in a court of law (Psalm 109:6), and playing the part of an adversary in general (Psalm 38:20). Nowhere in the Old Testament does Satan appear as a distinctive

[6] Buttrick A. George, "The Interpreters Dictionary of the Bible", Abingdon Press 1962. Vol.1 page 838, vol 4. page224-228

demonic figure, opposed to God and responsible for all evil. It is simply an appellative, not a proper name (i.e., it merely defines the role which the being in question happens to play in a particular situation).

The word *Satan* is from the Hebrew root *sin*, meaning "to block," "to attack," "to malign." The Old Testament term *devil* has its origin in Hebrew judicial terminology as the "adversary." It was this word *diabolos* that Jesus employed in John 6:70 when He said of Judas, "Have not I chosen you twelve, and one of you is a devil?" Note again that Jesus does not say one of them is possessed of a devil, but one of them is a devil.

A devil is a wicked man, not a spirit of evil that may possess a man or a monster whose all-pervading powers and influence may overcome him. Peter became a Satan by opposing Jesus; Judas became a devil by betraying his Master, and by allowing his covetousness to dominate him. And we ourselves become devils in the sight of God when we oppose the words of Jesus.

Bible Devils

Paul had a longing desire to visit his brethren at Thessalonica, and he wrote to them in the following manner: "Wherefore we would have come unto you, even I Paul, once and again; but Satan hindered us" (1 Thessalonians 2:18). Who obstructed Paul's travels? Perhaps it was a government official. Or it may have been a sect of the Jews; on several occasions they watched the gates of the city to take his life. Once they stoned him and left him for dead; at another time, forty men vowed that they would neither eat nor drink until they had taken his life. Any such Satan could have prevented his travel in this case, especially in the sense of the accuser at court (Zechariah 3:1). It is to be emphasized that the term "Satan hindered us" in the book of 1 Thessalonians 2:18 is not identified with Satan, the ruler of this world as some teach. This Satan was human and not of a supernatural origin. If this Satan was supernatural, how did Paul recognize him?

Much religious thinking and false teaching has attached to the word *devil* ideas that it was never meant to convey. The Bible itself does not teach the existence of a literal devil that tempts men to do wrong. False teaching has mystified the meaning of the original word and given countenance to pagan demonic theories that the Bible does not support.

In the Bible, the term *Satan* is applied to "an adversary, an opposer." Wicked men and women opposing God and His plans are called Satan. In Bible terminology the person performing evil is a Satan, a devil. In Matthew 10:23, Jesus showed clearly how a man becomes a devil: by opposing His words and being His adversary. Peter said to Jesus, "Lord, this shall not be unto thee." And Jesus said to him, "Get thee behind me, Satan: thou art an offense unto me." Peter became a Satan, an adversary of Jesus, by opposing His words.

The Strong's Greek word *diabolos* is the equivalent of the Hebrew *sin,* and it means "an accuser, calumniator," one who defames. But whoever this Satan may have been, of one thing we may be certain: it was not the devil of popular theology.

These same devils hindered Paul and Silas in their travels, when they cast them into the "inner prison" and made their feet fast in the stocks (Acts 16).

This same devil or agent of evil is spoken of in Revelation 2:10: "Behold, the devil shall cast some of you into prison, that ye may be tried." No monster from the infernal regions would have come forth to cast the followers of Jesus into prison cells. Nor would a disembodied evil spirit have such a power. The devil in this instance was someone with authority, someone who would oppose the religion of Jesus and had the power to open and close prison doors, as did Herod when he imprisoned John the Baptist.

God and the Devil

If we accept belief in a literal devil or power of evil, we are recognizing a second deity with a second dominion. In the divine record, the Bible, all power and all dominion are clearly and unmistakably ascribed to Jehovah and to Him alone. God is the great first cause and has no rivals. Through His prophet Isaiah, He says, "I am God, and there is none else; I am God, and there is none like me" (Isaiah 46:9). Also through His servant Moses,

He says, "Hear, O Israel: the Lord our God is one Lord" (Deuteronomy 6:4). He is the one, supreme God; He has no equal.

The Bible also speaks of devils, plural. There is only *one* God, and if He can have only one counterpart, then there is only *one* supreme cause of evil—singular, not plural. But we read in James 2:19, "The devils also believe and tremble." Let us identify one such devil. We find him alluded to in Acts 24:25. As the great apostle Paul "reasoned of righteousness, temperance, and judgment to come, Felix trembled." This devil trembled, but his devil nature was unrestrained; and when Paul offered him no money, "Felix, willing to show the Jews a pleasure, left Paul bound."

If we recognize a devil as a being of authority, he must have obtained that authority and power from the great Creator—for "there is no power but of God" (Romans 13:1). Why would a good and wise Creator give power to a being that would continually thwart his purposes and designs and perpetrate all manner of evil?

But no, God is the one and only God. He will not share His dominion with any other. "My glory will not I give to another" (Isaiah 42:8). If the theory of an all-powerful devil were true, then God would share His power with another. In fact, if that be the case, He much more than shares His glory with another, for the devil of popular belief gets ten adherents to the Almighty's one.

Sin Personified

The literary device known as personification is repeatedly employed in the Bible. For example, riches are personified in the following manner: "Ye cannot serve God and mammon" (Matthew 6:24). Wisdom is personified and termed *she*: "Happy is the man that findeth wisdom. She is more precious than rubies. Length of days is in her right hand; and in her left hand riches and honor" (Proverbs 3:13–17). Again she is represented as a "tree of life to them that lay hold upon her" (Proverbs 3:18). "Wisdom is justified of all her children" (Luke 7:35), a clear case of personification.

Sin is also personified and termed a master. In Romans 6, this device is employed a number of times: "Let not sin therefore reign in your mortal body, that ye should obey it in the lusts thereof ... For sin shall not have dominion over you. Know ye not, that to whom ye yield yourselves servants to obey, his servants ye are to whom ye obey; whether of sin unto death, or of obedience unto righteousness? But God be thanked, that [though] ye were the servants of sin ye have obeyed from the heart that form of doctrine which was delivered you. For when ye were the servants of sin, ye were free from righteousness" (Romans 6:12, 14, 16–17, and 20). Again, "Whosoever committeth sin is the servant of sin" (John 8:34; see also 1 John 3:8).

By means of personification, sin is also termed *devil* or *Satan*. When Jesus said to the Jews of His time, "Ye are of your father the devil, and the lusts of your father ye will do" (John 8:44), He also was employing this type of personification. He said, in effect, "Ye are of your fathers, a generation of evil men." Shortly before, John the Baptist had styled them a "generation of vipers." But no one would suppose he meant a generation of literal snakes!

When Ananias and his wife, Sapphira, sold a possession, keeping back part of the price, Peter questioned Ananias, "Why hath Satan filled thine heart to lie to the Holy Spirit?" (Acts3:1-10). Then three hours later Sapphira, not knowing of her husband's judicial death, came with the same story about the sale of the property. To her Peter said, "How is it that ye have agreed together to tempt the Spirit of the Lord?" The "Satan" that had filled their hearts was their own evil devices. They had agreed together to lie to the Lord. If an all-powerful being called "Satan" was the instigator of the lie, then the Lord showed criminal unfairness. He let the deceiver himself escape unharmed while punishing the deceived by killing them.

Paul describes this same Satan, or devil, sin personified, in Acts 26:16–18. Repeating the words that he had heard from Jesus at the time of his miraculous conversion, he says, "Rise, and stand upon thy feet: for I have appeared unto thee for this purpose, ... delivering thee from the people and from the Gentiles, unto whom now I send thee, to open their eyes, and to turn them from darkness to light, and from the power of Satan unto God, that they may receive forgiveness of sins, and inheritance among them which are sanctified by faith that is in me."

The author of the book of Hebrews also reveals who is the devil of the Bible. In Hebrews 2:14, speaking of Christ, he says, "that through death he might destroy him that had the power of death, that is, the devil." Now if we can find any statement about, what has the power of death, by it we can identify the devil, for that is one of his special features. "The sting of death is sin"

(1 Corinthians 15:56). *"The sting of death is sin."* Here we have the same answer that we obtain from Hebrews 2:14. *Sin* and the *devil* are synonymous terms. The devil has the power of death, and sin has the sting of death; hence, sin and all sinners compose the devil. In Zechariah 3, Joshua, the high priest, is represented as standing before the angel of the Lord, and Satan, this same devil, the personification of evil, is at his right hand to resist him. Here is a situation that every earnest life-seeker has experienced. As the apostle Paul wrote of his personal conflict, "That which I do I allow not: for what I would, that do I not; but what I hate, that do I. I find then a law, that, when I would do good, evil is present with me. For I delight in the law of God after the inward man: but I see another law in my members, warring against the law of my mind, and bringing me into captivity to the law of sin which is in my members" (Romans 7:15–23).

The Genesis Devil

Our earliest record of sin is in the first book of the Bible. Adam and Eve, representative of those whom God calls to serve Him, are placed in the garden of Eden, the spiritual field or vineyard of the Lord, where they must obey and live—or disobey and die. But at the enticement of the serpent, their own evil desires, they partake of the forbidden fruit and receive the consequent punishment for their sin. Disobedience was of their own choosing.

Here is one interpretation of the story of Adam and Eve, which we believe to be the correct Biblical interpretation, although not all religious groups agree.

According to the majority of Protestant and Catholic faiths, the devil began his work at what is called the *fall*, or the war in heaven. God placed Adam and Eve in the garden of Eden, a perfect world, free of sin, disease, and even death, where they might have lived on forever in perfect health and happiness had they not disobeyed the divine injunction: "Of every tree of the garden thou mayest freely eat: but of the tree of the knowledge of good and evil, thou shalt not eat of it: for in the day that thou eatest thereof thou shalt surely die."(Geneses 2:16-17)

But also in the garden was a serpent, a wily, subtle serpent who deceived Eve with these enticing words: "Ye shall not surely die: for God doth know that in the day ye eat thereof, then your eyes shall be opened, and ye shall be as gods, knowing good and evil" (Genesis 3:4–5). The forbidden fruit *did* look tempting; and yielding to the serpent's enticement, Eve partook. And she "gave also unto her husband with her; and he did eat."

What was the result of this transgression, according to theology? We quote from a typical Protestant constitution:

> Our first parents, being seduced by the subtlety and temptation of Satan, sinned in eating the forbidden fruit. This, their sin, God was pleased according to his wise and holy counsel, to permit, having purposed to order it to his own glory.
>
> By this sin they fell from their original righteousness and communion with God, and so became dead in sin and wholly defiled in all the faculties and parts of soul and body. They being the loot of all mankind, the guilt of this sin were imputed, and the same death in sin and corrupted nature conveyed to all their posterity, descending from them by ordinary generation.

A penalty of death passed upon Adam and Eve and all their posterity. Assuming that all mankind are descendants of Adam, they teach that this one transgression or "original sin" condemned the whole human race, and therefore all men are sinners and subject to death.

However, this is not the teaching of the Bible. Physical death was in the world long before the death of Adam, as is evidenced by the prehistoric remains of men and animals. The death to which Adam was condemned was not natural death, the result of mortality, but penal death, condemnation at judgment, eternal death. His receiving the disapproval of God did not change his physical nature from immortal to mortal.

Furthermore, the guilt of sin is not inherited. God does not condemn us for the sin of our father, our grandfather, or our greatest-greatest-greatest-grandfather Adam. Every person is responsible for his own sin. The divine principle is plain: "The fathers shall not die for the children; neither shall the children die for the fathers, but every man shall die for his own sin" (2 Chronicles 25:4). "Everyone shall die for his own iniquity: every man that eateth the sour grape, his teeth shall be set on edge" (Jeremiah 31:30). "Every man shall be put to death for his own sin" (2 Kings 14:6; also Deuteronomy 24:16).

Every man shall die for his own sin, not for Adam's sin. "The soul that sinneth, it shall die" (Ezekiel 18:20). It shall die, and no other. All mankind are not condemned as a result of Adam's transgression. The fall of man is a doctrine totally unscriptural.

—— The Serpent in the Garden of Eden ——

According to the Genesis narrative, the serpent was responsible for this disastrous "fall of man." But was this serpent the devil? Who or what tempted Eve to eat of the forbidden fruit?

To understand this serpent, we must recognize that the first three chapters of Genesis are not a story of literal events. Instead, they are an allegory, a symbolic representation and outline of God's plan for the redemption of mankind. Genesis is a story of symbols and shadows of things to come.

Following the Bible rule to compare spiritual things with spiritual (1 Corinthians 2:13), we see Adam and Eve not as the first man and woman to live on earth, but as the first man and woman called to work in the spiritual vineyard or garden of the Lord (Isaiah 5:7) for the reward of life eternal. "Early in the morning," early in the day of salvation (2 Corinthians 6:2), the Lord went out to hire laborers to work in this spiritual vineyard (Matthew 20:1–7). Thus Adam and Eve are representative of those men and women down through the ages whom God calls to serve Him. They are children of God (1 John 3:1) in the process of development. They are told to obey the commands of the Lord, but they often yield to temptation and transgress.

What tempts them to do wrong was not a literal serpent. No, they are tempted in the same manner as you and I: "Every man is tempted, when he is drawn away of his own lust and enticed" (James 1:14). Every man, Adam and Eve and all of their posterity are tempted "when he is drawn away of his own lust, and enticed."

Man is a generic term referring to both men and women, and James says that men are tempted by their own lust. Eve was tempted in like manner. Her own desires, not a crawling serpent, tempted her. The subtle serpent, which was "more subtle than any beast of the field," was her own human heart, which, says Jeremiah 17:9, is "deceitful above all things, and desperately wicked." When Eve saw the forbidden fruit of the tree—fruits of the flesh, "adultery, fornication, uncleanness, lasciviousness, idolatry, witchcraft, hatred, variance, emulations, wrath, strife, and such like" (Galatians 5:19–21)—she let her lust conceive. She allowed her desires to lead her, rather than obeying the divine command. And then, "When lust hath conceived, it bringeth forth sin: and sin, when it is finished, bringeth forth death" (James 1:15).

The apostle Paul tells us just how Eve was tempted. We may know how the serpent tempted Eve if we know how easily our own minds are corrupted by the promptings of our evil hearts. "But I fear, lest by any means, as the serpent beguiled Eve through his subtlety, so your minds should be corrupted from the simplicity that is in Christ."(2 Corinthians11:3)

The minds of the people of the church at Corinth were corrupted from the simplicity of the doctrine of Christ by their own tendency to cling to their former beliefs and notions. Our minds are corrupted in the same manner today.

And this is how Eve was beguiled by the talk of the serpent. She listened to the promptings of her own mind. There was no more a literal serpent in the garden of Eden than there is in our hearts now. Adam and Eve, as representative of all covenant makers, simply wanted their own way and were led astray from single-hearted devotion to God by their own fleshly minds. There is nothing here to suggest a supernatural fallen being as the problem.

Enmity Between the Two Seeds

In the Genesis allegory, we read further of enmity between the woman and the serpent. "And I will put enmity between thee and the woman and between thy seed and her seed; it shall bruise thy head, and thou shalt bruise his heel."(Geneses 3:15) What are the two seeds? Would the Lord be talking about enmity between the children of the literal woman and the offspring of the literal serpent? What foolishness!

But enmity has always existed between the children of light and the children of darkness and evil. We read, "Wisdom is justified of all her children" (Luke 7:35) and "Ye are all the children of light, we are not of the night, nor of darkness" (1 Thessalonians 5:5). Enmity exists between those who walk as children of light, or the seed of the woman, and those who walk after the flesh, governed by the serpent nature. This has nothing to do with a devil seed and a God seed. Some believe this to be Eve giving birth to Satan's child.

Let us look at the first case of enmity related in the divine record, the enmity that existed between Cain and Abel. The apostle John tells us the cause of this enmity: "Not as Cain, who was of that wicked one, and slew his brother. And wherefore slew he him? Because his own works were evil, and his brother's righteous." (1 John 3:12) Here was enmity between two seeds, an enmity that led to the death of one brother. The enmity was between a child of our mother, divine wisdom, and a child of the flesh, the serpent or devil that produces evil and sin fruits. The enmity has been the same through the ages: between Jeremiah and his persecutors, Daniel and his adversaries, Stephen and those who stoned him, and Jesus and those who betrayed Him.

We read further in the Genesis allegory: "It [the seed of the woman] shall bruise thy head, and thou shalt bruise his heel" (Genesis 3:15). The seed of the serpent bruises the "heel" of the seed of the woman. It does no vital damage to the seed, for such bruising cannot do eternal harm and affect its prospects of eternal life. The seed of the woman bruises the serpent on the head, and such harm is significant. The woman, the "Elect Lady and her children" (2 John 1:1), the faithful servants of God, will strike at the serpent's head—at the theories, the doctrines, the superstitions and errors, and all the evil that is perpetuating the serpent nature. Ultimately, sin and all sinners will forever cease to exist and "the earth shall be full of the knowledge of the Lord, as the waters cover the sea" (Isaiah 11:9). The crushing of the serpent's head will then be complete.

Devils That Tempt

Having identified the devil of the Bible as evil men and women, workers of iniquity, let us now study one of his best-known activities: temptation. Workers of evil have by their strong and ever-present influence repeatedly led nobler souls astray. The children of God were well acquainted with such devils even as far back as the time of Job.

Satan and Job

The presence of Satan in Job 1 is not definite proof that the scriptures uphold the idea of an all-powerful being with powers for evil capable of subduing God's powers for good. Indeed, such a position, if it could be proved, would seriously discredit the Almighty's claim to absolute fairness, to "justice and judgment," as attributed by the psalmist (Psalm 89:14).

Authorities on scripture agree that *Satan*, as used in Job 1, should be a proper name. In the *Complete Jewish Bible*, by David Stern, page 993 the word *Satan* is rendered "the Adversary."[7] *Satan*, in biblical usage, denotes anyone in opposition to God; it is a Hebrew word "signifying an adversary, an enemy, an accuser."(The companion Bible Page 667 margin footnotes)

In Job 1, the Satan maliciously tries to withdraw God's approval from Job by attributing low motives to him. The terms employed are those commonly used in a court of law, with Satan playing the role of "accuser" or "prosecuting attorney."

Knowing that in Bible phraseology the terms *Satan* and *devil* are invariably applied to men and women who oppose God and disobey His

---

[7] Stern, H. Stern, "The Complete Jewish Bible", Messianic Jewish publishers, Clarksville MD. Page 993. The companion Bible page 667 footnotes

law, we can more easily understand the Satan referred to in Job 1:6. "There was a day when the sons of God came to present themselves before the Lord, and Satan came also among them." This Satan was a representative individual, a man, not a demon or a man possessed by a demon.

Just as Judas was among the apostles who gathered with Jesus at the Last Supper before His crucifixion, so Satan was among these sons of God, or servants of God (1 John 3:2), who gathered in Job's day. Here is symbolized an ever-present truth: wherever God has servants, He also has enemies. The Bible speaks of Cain and Abel. Ten of the spies Moses sent to spy on the land of Canaan proved to be Satan's, adversaries to God's purpose, and they brought back an evil report, whereas only two brought back a favorable report. There were Elijah and Ahab, Samuel and Saul, King David and his erstwhile companion who at one time had been his guide and close acquaintance but who became his archenemy. Of him, David said, "We took sweet counsel together, and walked unto the house of God in company" (Psalm 55:12–14). Demas was even in the yoke with Paul, and then proved to be a traitor.

Wheat and tares grow together, sheep and goats share the same pastures, and righteous and wicked attend the same meetings. It was true in Job's day and in Jesus' day, and it is still true in our day. Wherever there are servants or sons of God, Satan, the adversary, is present.

It does not seem consistent with reason to suppose that the account in Job is a literal occurrence. It seems more fitting to view it as a poem, a parable, or a story containing the highest moral. Twice in the book of Job we read that "Job continued his parable" (Job 27:1, 29:1). It has been suggested that the purpose of the book of Job is to discuss the problem of life—and, in particular, to refute the popular idea that suffering is proof of sin, and that great suffering is proof of great sin.

To confirm our identification of Satan, let us not overlook the physical features of this Satan that was involved in the controversy about Job's sincerity. He appeared in person; he was able to walk, talk, and converse with the Lord. The devil of theology is not able to do all of these things.

The book of Job is part of the wisdom literature of the Bible, which includes Job, Proverbs, Ecclesiastes, and part of the Psalms. If we approach the book of Job from this angle, all the incongruities disappear. Job's boils and the potsherd with which he scraped himself are indicative of the evils of the flesh that defile us, and of the vital willingness on our part to be cleansed from them, whatever the process.

Satan, likewise, is representative. Our evil natures are always ready to discredit our brother on the ground that his service for God is a shrewd bargain that he serves for the temporal advantages he gains in so doing. And God, in His unimpeachable justice and fair dealing with His earthly children, is the hero of the story. (We will discuss Job's experience with Satan again later.)

—— Who Hardened Pharaoh's Heart? ——

Is the devil a spirit of evil? Seven times we are told that the Lord hardened Pharaoh's heart, and three times that he hardened his own heart. Once we are told that it was God's leniency that prompted him to harden his heart. Exodus 8:15 lists this once-mentioned instance: "But when Pharaoh saw that there was respite, he hardened his heart, and hearkened not unto them, as the Lord had said." One text, the word of the Philistine lords, specifically says that Pharaoh hardened his own heart: "Wherefore then do ye harden your hearts, as the Egyptians and Pharaoh hardened their hearts, when he wrought wonderfully among them" (1 Samuel 6:6).

Pharaoh was a tool in performing the Lord's purpose, but his action was entirely of his own volition. Every man is a free moral agent, free to choose his own course of action. God has the power to foreknow what that action will be, and therefore He is able to fit that action into His overall divine plan.

— Who Provoked David to Number Israel? —

Some organizations hold to the belief that the devil is a super being capable of provoking men to evil. However, such a theory cannot be the truth of the matter, because it flatly contradicts other plain Biblical statements.

If a super being called Satan stood up against Israel and provoked King David to number the people in defiance of God's orders, then Jesus told an untruth when He said that nothing from outside a man can defile him

(Mark 7:20–23). And James also would be mistaken when he said that "every man is tempted when he is drawn away of his own lust, and enticed," if a literal super powerful devil can tempt men to do wrong.

To be sure, something provoked David to sin. Was it he himself, or someone else? The king's order was abominable to Joab, the chief captain of the army; hence he could not have influenced David to take the census. And there is no record of any other person influencing the king. We will let David speak for himself: "Is it not I that commanded the people to be numbered? Even I it is that have sinned and done evil indeed" (1 Chronicles 21:17).

David's own ungoverned pride was the Satan in the case; his own desire to know how great the nation under him had become prompted him to number the people. The Satan who enticed David was his own human ego, his frailty and weakness.

Who Tempted Jesus?

The temptation of Jesus is frequently used to prove the existence of a literal, personal devil. A moment's reflection, however, dissipates this impression. If Judas could be a devil and yet a man, why could not the tempter of Jesus be a man? His being called a devil proves nothing, for a devil in the person of Herod cast John the Baptist into prison. Devils in the Bible were men, not monsters or spirits or demons acting as God's counterpart.

When a devil in the person of a former Herod heard that Jesus was born in Bethlehem, "he was greatly troubled." In fact, he became so enraged when he could not find the child that he sent "and slew all the children that were in Bethlehem, and in all the coasts thereof, from two years old and under."(Matthew 2:16) Was he not an extremely cruel devil?

What caused him to be so bitter against the baby Jesus? The conviction was widespread that the Messiah, the heir to the throne of David, was to be born. And Herod, fearing for his own authority, sought to end the life of the youthful heir, but Jesus' family escaped. Thirty years later, Jesus, having reached the age when He was to begin His great mission, stepped forth from His secluded home in Nazareth to perform mighty signs and wonders.

The tradition of the Messiah who should put down all kings on earth and exalt Himself as universal ruler was spreading, and at the time of His temptation. The fame of Jesus as the claimant to the Messiahship was also beginning to be known. A different Herod was in power, but do you not suppose that he was aware of the events of thirty years earlier and wished to make terms with this rapidly rising star in Judea? The devil or tempter, in this case, was most certainly Herod or someone of authority acting as his representative.

Have we any substantial evidence for this position? Let us examine each aspect of the incident. Jesus' enemy or tempter did not understand that the prophecies concerning the Messiah, who was to put down all kings of earth and be exalted as universal ruler, were not to be fulfilled until Christ's second coming. Therefore, he endeavored to induce Jesus to pay him homage.

The first temptation concerned Jesus' ability to make bread of stones, or the temptation of material success. Jesus didn't need to go hungry, then or ever. He could have built a prosperous business and acquired comfort and wealth, but should He? That was the temptation.

The second temptation concerned authority. Every aspiring young man craves authority, and Jesus was no exception. "Then the Devil taketh Him up into the Holy City and setteth him on a Pinnacle of the temple." (Matthew 4:5). We may wonder how he could take Jesus to the pinnacle of the temple, because it would require more than human power to transport a man through the air to the top of a tall steeple. But the pinnacle of the temple, as we are informed by Josephus, was an elevated court or promenade, which on one side overlooked the valley of Jehoshaphat.

The enemy also took Jesus up on a high mountain, so that His field of vision was in proportion to the altitude. The tract of country seen would have been Judea, and the offer of power would relate to that country.

How can we know that this tempter was a Roman prince or agent of Herod, someone with authority? Because he had the power to allot the provinces of the Roman Empire: "All these things will I give thee, if thou wilt fall down and worship me" (Matthew 4:8). Furthermore, this devil or enemy tempting Jesus could walk and talk and was visible to the eye. He was a real being, as real as the devils of today, men and women in every avenue of life who try to lead others in the ways of sin to destruction.

The devil and the temptations were real. The offer of a high position in this world would be a temptation to almost any man, and Jesus was "in all points tempted like as we are, yet without sin" (Hebrews 4:15). To Jesus, with His superior abilities, the offer of power was a temptation, but He did not yield. In each instance, He had the ready answer: "It is written."

— Who Was the Devil That Sowed Tares? —

In His parable of the tares, as related in Matthew 13, Jesus describes another of the devil's mischievous designs. An enemy sowed tares in a wheat field. After Jesus had sent the multitude away, He explained the parable to His disciples.

"He said unto them, he that soweth the good seed is the Son of man; the field is the world; the good seed are the children of the kingdom; but the tares are the children of the wicked one; and the enemy who sowed them is the devil" (Matthew 13:37–39). The word *one* does not appear in the original Greek manuscript. Two modern versions read "the weeds are the wicked" and "the tares are the sons of evil."

Like kind, begets like kind. If the tares are the sons of evil, the devil that sowed them must be a father of evil. The answer is obvious: the devil represents evil men.

— What Devil Contended with Michael? —

According to verse 9 of Jude, a certain devil caused a serious contention with the archangel Michael in the days of Moses. Who was this devil?

We cannot believe the inspired Word depicts any altercation between a literal devil and an angel over the physical body of Moses when he died on lonely Mount Nebo. Moses was buried by the angels, with no man knowing the place of his burial to this day. How dare we interpret this occurrence to say that a corporate devil or Satan contended with an archangel over Moses's body at the time of his burial?

In view of plain Bible teaching about devils, what could be the meaning of verse 9 of Jude? Why should we suppose that the contention was over the physical body of Moses at his prearranged demise on Mount Nebo? The short account in Deuteronomy 34 contains no suggestion of such an experience.

Here's a more realistic approach to the meaning of verse 9 of Jude, which does not conflict with the general teaching of the Bible. Moses, as the archangel, *contended*—*argued* or *debated*, as translated in newer versions of the Bible—with the devil Pharaoh over the freeing of the children of Israel, who were Moses's followers.

How does this approach fit into the picture? *Michael* means "one like God." Can we ascertain that Moses was in God's place or like Him when the children of Israel were saved from Egypt? Yes, we can. "And the Lord said unto Moses, 'See, I have made thee a god to Pharaoh: and Aaron thy brother shall be thy prophet. Thou shalt speak all that I command thee: and Aaron thy brother shall speak unto Pharaoh, that he sends the children of Israel out of this land'" (Exodus 7:1). We learn from this testimony that Moses was seen as god by Pharaoh, or was to act with authority. Again in Exodus 4:16, the Lord, speaking of Aaron, says to Moses, "And he shall be thy spokesman unto the people: and he shall be to thee instead of a mouth, and thou shalt be to him instead of God." Moses was acting in God's place; he was the Michael, the one like God, to Pharaoh.

But who was the adversary or devil? Certainly Moses's great adversary in this transaction was Pharaoh, who was strongly opposed to God. Moses's constant cry to Pharaoh was, "Thus saith the Lord, Let my people go, that they may serve me." Michael (Moses), acting in God's place, went to Pharaoh to demand that he let the people go, so clearly Pharaoh was the devil.

Who is represented by the *body* that caused the contention between Michael, acting in God's place, and Pharaoh, the great adversary? Any reasonable person would at once answer that it was the children of Israel. A military commander often refers to his troops as a *body*, and the church is called Christ's body (1 Corinthians 12:27; Ephesians 1:23). Similarly, Israel would have been Moses's body.

Are Devils Fallen Angels?

Is it possible that God would ask us to believe that one who is found worthy of becoming a holy angel and being clothed with immortality, one who has become "holy and without blemish," could rebel against the eternal creator who had lifted him to glory and eternal life? If an angel could fall from such an exalted position, what assurance would you or I have that after spending our lives developing the character God desires and receiving God's approval for our efforts, a similar cataclysm might not overtake us?

But no, such a thing is unthinkable—impossible and unscriptural. If we can rebel after being saved and given immortality, then the promise of Isaiah 45:17 is untrue: "But Israel shall be saved in the Lord with an everlasting salvation: ye shall not be ashamed nor confounded world without end." Our salvation is everlasting, and we are in no danger of falling.

Yet various groups of religious-minded people believe that devils were once bright angels around the throne of glory in the high courts of heaven. To support this position, they frequently turn to Isaiah 14 for evidence. Verse 12 reads, "How art thou fallen from heaven, O Lucifer, son of the morning! How art thou cut down to the ground, which didst weaken the nations?"

Who Was Lucifer?

Harper's Bible Dictionary Harper Collins New York, N.Y.1985 ed. page 582 says of the name *Lucifer*, as used in Isaiah 14:12, "Used to render the Hebrew 'shining one' applied to the King of Babylon, fallen from his high estate. In the third century A.D. the saying of Jesus: 'I beheld Satan as lightning fall from heaven' (Luke 10:18) was erroneously supposed to refer to Isaiah 14:12. Hence, Lucifer came to be regarded as the name of Satan before his fall." Not until the third century was Lucifer regarded as Satan.

The context in Isaiah 14:12 make it very plain who this Lucifer was, and from what heaven he fell. We are told in Isaiah 14:4 that, "Thou shalt take up this proverb against the king of Babylon, and say, how hath the oppressor ceased! The golden city ceased!" This narrative is a proverb directed against the king of Babylon, and no one else. The proverb continues in the following verses, still referring to the deposed and slain king of Babylon, until verse 12, where the taunt is flung (some commentators style it a taunt-song): "How art thou fallen from heaven, O Lucifer, son of the morning! How art thou cut down to the ground, which didst weaken the nations?"

Verses 13 and 14 continue: "Thou hast said in thine heart, I will ascend into heaven, I will exalt my throne above the stars of God: I will also sit upon the mount of the congregation, in the sides of the north: I will ascend above the heights of the clouds; I will be like the most High."

When the king of Babylon said in his heart, "I will ascend into heaven," he was not necessarily speaking of the physical heaven. When he said, "I will exalt myself above the stars of God," he was not speaking of the stars that shine in the firmament on a dark night. He was

saying, "I will exalt myself above the other political leaders in my realm." He was determined to exalt himself above the "stars" or kings in their immediate realm, Jerusalem, their seat of government, and make them his satellites, as demonstrated in the following sentence: "I will sit also upon the mount of the congregation, in the sides of the north." Jerusalem, the seat of secular and religious authority, is indicated here. Jerusalem is similarly identified in Psalm 48:1–2: "Great is the Lord, and greatly to be praised in the city of our God, in the mountain of his holiness. Beautiful for situation, the joy of the whole earth, is mount Zion, on the sides of the north, the city of the great King."

The term *heaven* is used elsewhere in the following scriptures of the political leadership: "Hear, O heavens, and give ear, O earth: for the Lord hath spoken," and "Hear the word of the Lord, ye rulers of Sodom; give ear unto the law of our God, ye people of Gomorrah" (Isaiah 1:2 and 10).

Isaiah 14:10 also clearly identifies Lucifer as a man: "They that see thee shall narrowly look upon thee, and consider thee, saying, is this, the man that made the earth to tremble, that did shake kingdoms?" Lucifer was the king of Babylon. He fell from heaven, his seat of authority and power, and became as weak as the common people. Could anything be plainer than this, when we let the Almighty use His own qualifying terms?

Who Was the Cherub of Ezekiel 28?

Was the cherub of Ezekiel 28 the likeness of Lucifer or in any way related to the devil? Verses 1 and 2 read, "The word of the Lord came again unto me, saying, Son of man, say unto the prince of Tyrus, Thus saith the Lord God." The word of the Lord was being directed to "the prince of Tyrus" in its immediate context. The word *Tyrus* is defined as "an adversary, an enemy reserved for the Day of Judgment and vengeance." (The companion Bible margin page 1145, 12-17)The prince of Tyrus, in a spiritual sense, includes those who prove unfaithful or become enemies of God, those whom God will bring to judgment to "convince all that are ungodly among them of all their ungodly deeds which they have ungodly committed, and of all their hard speeches which ungodly sinners have spoken against him. These are murmurs, complainers, walking after their own lusts; and their mouth speaketh great swelling words, having men's persons in admiration because of advantage" (Jude v. 15–16).

Ezekiel says further: "Thus saith the Lord God: Because thine heart is lifted up, and thou hast said, I am a god, I sit in the seat of God, in the midst of the seas; yet thou art a man, and not God, though thou set thine heart as the heart of God."(Ezekiel 28:2)

Verse 12 contains more of this message: "Thus saith the Lord God; Thou sealest up the sum, full of wisdom, and perfect in beauty. Thou hast been in Eden the garden of God; every precious stone was thy covering." The persons represented here had been in Eden, the vineyard or garden of the Lord, where all of God's servants labor during their day of salvation. As servants of God, they had been heir to God's richest blessings, eternal life, but they did not choose to submit themselves to the rule of God.

"Thou art the anointed cherub that covereth; and I have set thee so: thou wast upon the holy mountain of God; thou hast walked up and down in the midst of the stones of fire. Thou wast perfect in thy ways from the day that thou wast created, till iniquity was found in thee" (Ezekiel 28:14–15). The situation of these people is the same as that of the Galatians' brethren, to whom Paul wrote many years later, "Ye did run well; who did hinder you that ye should not obey the truth?" (Galatians 5:7).

What will be the result of their disobedience? "Therefore will I bring forth a fire from the midst of thee, it shall devour thee, and I will bring thee to ashes upon the earth in the sight of all them that behold thee" (verse 18). Fire, representing the judgment of God, shall devour them, and "never shalt thou be any more" (verse 19).

No, the cherub does not represent the devil—a monster, evil spirit, demon, or fallen angel—but only unfaithful servants of God who could have received God's high honors and blessings for faithfulness, but who proved disloyal to their trust, thus becoming subject to God's judgment.

What Angels "Kept Not Their First Estate"?

If devils are not angels fallen from heaven, who are the "angels which kept not their first estate, but left their own habitation" (Jude v. 6)?

Jude writes of a particular event in history: "I will therefore put you in remembrance, though ye once knew this, how that the Lord, having saved the people out of the land of Egypt, afterward destroyed them that believed not" (verse 5). Notice particularly that Jude wishes us to recall something that occurred when the Lord saved His people out of Egypt. Jude is not calling our attention to something that happened up in heaven, but to what happened when God saved the people out of the land of Egypt.

Verse 6 continues, "And the angels which kept not their first estate, but left their own habitation, he hath reserved in everlasting chains under darkness unto the judgment of the great day." First let us ask, who were these angels? What is the meaning of the word *angel*?

*Liddell and Scott's *Greek-English Lexicon, Oxford University Press, Oxford, by Stanford, David 1987 page 2-3* defines the word *angelos*, translated as "angels" in Jude, as "messengers, envoy, generally one that announces or tells." The term may refer either to mortal or immortal messengers. What kind of messengers was Jude speaking about? They were messengers serving in the days when the Lord saved His people out of the land of Egypt.

When Israel first came to the borders of the Promised Land, about two years after their departure from Egypt, "the Lord spake unto Moses, saying, Send thou men that they may search the land of Canaan, which I give unto the children of Israel: of every tribe of their fathers shall ye send a man, everyone a ruler among them" (Numbers 13:2). Here were twelve men, rulers among them, men high in authority, chosen to be messengers sent into the land of Canaan. Moses sent them to spy out the land and bring back an account of it.

After forty days the messengers returned from their search, bringing with them luscious grapes, pomegranates, and figs. Ten of these messengers brought also an evil report of the land (Numbers 13:32), which caused a mass rebellion among the Israelites, turning them against Moses and Aaron. Eight of the spies turned against Caleb and Joshua, who refused to consent with their evil report. "And the men which Moses sent to search the land, who returned and made all the congregation murmur against him, by bringing up a slander upon the land, even those men died by the plague before the Lord" (Numbers 14:36–37). These messengers were Jews who fell from their high estate when God delivered His people from Egypt.

Each of these men had been a ruler in his own tribe, but because of their disobedience they fell and became "reserved unto the day of judgment." Neither Jude nor any other Bible author ever taught that angels—glorified, immortal beings—can fall from the heaven where God dwells. But when we let the Bible interpret itself, all is plain.

Jesus Beheld Satan Fall

When the seventy disciples whom Jesus sent forth had returned, having accomplished their mission, Jesus "said unto them, I beheld Satan as lightning fall from heaven" (Luke 10:18). Who was the Satan that He was talking about? Satan, as we have discussed already, may be used as the personification of evil and sin. Revelation assures us that all sinners are doomed for eventual destruction in the "lake of fire which is the second death" (Revelation 20:9–10 and 14; 21:8).

When Jesus said He "beheld Satan as lightning fall from heaven," He spoke prophetically. The heaven this Satan now occupies is not God's heaven, but the social and political heavens of our troubled cosmos. But Satan will fall from it, be cast out, when Christ and His co-rulers take the reins of government and suppress all evil. During the millennial reign, sin and all sinners will be bound, and at the close of the millennium they will be eliminated. Satan will fall from heaven, the high places of the government of the world, and sin shall lose its last dominion on earth forever. The Hebrew word for Satan is *adversary* and when used correctly from the Hebrew text, it clearly refers not to a supernatural being but to an adversary of a human.

What Devils Did Jesus Cast Out?

On several occasions during Jesus' ministry, He was said to cast out devils. An outstanding example of this was Jesus' healing the insane man (Luke 8:26–34). The devils were said to have left the insane man and entered into a herd of swine.

Knowing that the word *devil* is used to refer to an opposer, as when Peter opposed Jesus in Matthew 16:23, we can understand that a devil might also refer to something that opposes a healthy condition of body or mind. In the Gospels, diseases are often called devils. The Greek word employed is *daimonion,* meaning "demon."

Verse 29 reveals that the man was insane: "For He had commanded the unclean spirit to come out of the man, for oftentimes it had caught him: and he was kept bound with chains and in fetters; and he would break the bands, and was driven of the devil into the wilderness." The word used here is *daimon,* meaning "a deified spirit" (of a bad nature).

"And Jesus asked him, saying, what is thy name? And he said, Legion: because many devils were entered into him. And they be sought Him that He would not command them to go out into the deep" (verses 30–31). Here we see the confused thinking of an insane man, who thought of himself as a dual personality, or "legion."

In verses 32 and 33, the insane man, thinking himself to be many in one, implored Jesus that the disease might leave him and go into the swine, and Jesus did so. He had the power to cure the insane man, but also the ability to infect the swine with the mental disturbance that had afflicted the man, with the result that the swine ran into the lake and drowned.

Verse 35 shows that the man was definitely insane: "Then they [the people of the nearby village] went out to see what was done; and came to Jesus, and found the man, out of whom the devils were departed, sitting at the feet of Jesus, clothed, and in his right mind." The man was now in his right mind. He had been insane, and Jesus had healed the insanity, known as a devil.

In Matthew 12:43–45, Jesus spoke a parable that may have been suggested by the case history of another insane man. In this case, the man, who was thought to have been cured, suffered a relapse, and his condition became even worse. "When the unclean spirit is gone out of a man, He walketh through dry places, seeking rest, and findeth none. Then He saith, I will return into my house from whence I came out; and when He is come, He findeth it empty, swept, and garnished. Then goeth he, and taketh with himself seven other spirits more wicked than himself, and they enter in and dwell there: and the last state of that man is worse than the first."

The lesson in this parable concerns the persistence of wickedness. When the soul is not indwelt by the rightful tenant, righteousness is always beleaguered and wickedness returns. Rejection of evil is never enough; at best, it is only a prelude to a new loyalty. Nature and human nature both abhor a vacuum: no faith is almost worse than a bad faith, for no faith invites a swarm of bad faiths. No life remains empty of worship. It doesn't help a man to know what he does *not* believe, unless he knows also what he *does* believe.

The Pharisees had cast out the gross sins, but they left life empty of any loyalty beyond themselves. So seven other "devils" arrived, in the form of love of money, greed, self-righteousness, and hypocrisy. In this parable, our Lord was foretelling the degeneration of people who imagine that they have nothing to learn from Him, although He has more wisdom to impart than Solomon gave to the queen of Sheba.

Resisting the Devil

"Resist the devil, and he will flee from you," commanded the practical James (4:7). Who or what is this devil? Can we identify him? Is he a real corporeal enemy? On D-day during World War II, if the Allied forces landing on the beachhead of Normandy had found no enemy, met no opposition, what a strange situation it would have been! Or, to make the metaphor still more ridiculous, if they had known nothing about the type of fighting men they were to encounter—nothing of their armaments or their ability to fight, nothing of their maneuverability or their possible war strategy—what a predicament they would have been in!

But that is just the position we are in today in our religious life, if the beliefs of much of the religious world are true. The devil of popular belief is sometimes said to be heavily armed, but we have never been shown one piece of his armament. He is said to have a personality of his own, but we have never seen one hair of his head. He must have a voice, for he is said to go about as a roaring lion "seeking whom he may devour," but we have never heard a faint whisper from him in our ear during our entire lives.

People who would lay the blame for evil and sin on an imaginary devil will fail, because they are fighting something that does not exist—and neglecting the real devils, the evil within their own hearts. These devils, said Jesus, come from within the human mind and "defile the man."

The pagan world of Paul's time believed in demons and spirits; some groups thought of the heavenly bodies as the abodes of spirits that hold human life in thrall. Paul himself espoused no such beliefs, but he did borrow from the language of contemporary astrology to describe the conflict between good and evil. For example, he wrote, "For we wrestle not against flesh and blood, but against principalities, against powers, against the rulers of the darkness of this world, against spiritual wickedness in high places" (Ephesians 6:12). He spoke also of "the prince of the power of the air," referring again to the powers of evil. In this way, he was expressing to the Gentiles, in language they could understand, the very real and earnest Christian conflict with all powers of sin and evil which every Christian must experience.

God Provides Armor

God has not left us defenseless against the devil—all sin and evil—but has provided strong, tested spiritual armor. "Put on the whole armor of God," advises the apostle Paul, "that ye may be able to stand against the wiles of the devil" (Ephesians 6:11). Then he names each essential piece of this God-given armor: "Stand therefore, having your loins girt about with truth, and having on the breastplate of righteousness; and your feet shod with the preparation of the gospel of peace; above all, taking the shield of faith, wherewith ye shall be able to quench all the fiery darts of the wicked. And take the helmet of salvation, and the sword of the Spirit, which is the word of God" (Ephesians 6:14–17). These are weapons with which to fight against wicked people, not corporeal devils.

What Do We Fight?

Paul did not spend his time warning people against a literal devil or blaming evil on an external power, nor did he himself fight in that kind of warfare. Paul knew *whom* he was fighting, and he also knew *why* he was fighting. The battle he was fighting gave him the blessed assurance that a crown of glory would be his at the coming of the Master. He affirmed with confidence, "I therefore so run, not as uncertainly; so fight I, not as one that beateth the air." Whom did he fight against? "I keep under my body, and bring it into subjection; lest that by any means, when I have preached to others, I myself should be a castaway" (1 Corinthians 9:26–27). He fought to bring his body into subjection, "casting down imaginations, and every high thing that exalteth itself against the knowledge of God, and bringing into captivity every thought to the obedience of Christ" (2 Corinthians 10:4–5). By such fighting as this, Paul defeated the devil within himself.

To resist the devil means simply to conquer one's own self—a great accomplishment, for he who can rule himself is greater than "he that taketh a city" (Proverbs 16:32). Jesus said clearly what we must war against: "There is nothing from without a man, that entering into him can defile him: but the things which come out of him, those are they that defile the man …_For from within, out of the heart of men, proceed evil thoughts, adulteries, fornications, murders, thefts, covetousness, wickedness, deceit, lasciviousness, an evil eye, blasphemy, pride, foolishness: all these evil things come from within, and defile the man" (Mark 7:14–15, 21–23). All these evil things come from *within* and defile the man. Nothing outside a man can defile him by entering into him—*nothing*, whether devil or spirit or power of any kind. A man can be defiled only when his own mind give its consent. This unequivocal statement leaves absolutely no place for the demoralizing work of the devil.

The Future of the Devil

Today the devil (i.e., workers of evil and iniquity) runs unrestrained. "The heart of the sons of men is fully set in them to do evil" (Ecclesiastes 8:11). The prophet Micah foretold this condition, that men would "do evil with both hands earnestly" (Micah 7:3). However, this condition will not always prevail. Christ is coming to establish a new government of righteousness and equity. He is coming to put down evil, exalt righteousness, and become Earth's rightful king (Zechariah 14:9).

How will these promises be realized? When Christ comes, not all men will readily accept Him in this capacity of absolute ruler. The devil, the evil in men's hearts, will come forward, and all nations shall rise up and resist Him. The prophet Daniel foretold the struggle that would ensue, calling it a time of trouble "such as never was since there was a nation even to that same time" (Daniel 12:1). The revelator describes this same struggle between the forces of Christ and the powers of evil as the war in heaven.

The War in Heaven

Speaking prophetically, the revelator writes, "And there appeared a great wonder in heaven; a woman clothed with the sun and the moon under her feet and upon her head a crown of twelve stars" (Revelation 12:1). Could anyone for a moment imagine this to be a literal woman, clothed with the literal sun (864,100 miles in diameter), the literal moon under her feet, and stars upon her head? What nonsense!

An understanding of this passage in accord with the other teachings of the Bible might run like this. A spiritual woman is spoken of in Luke 7:35: "Wisdom is justified of all her children." This woman is the truth of God personified, represented as enveloped in light, the light of Christ, the sun of righteousness (Malachi 4:2). She is standing on the moon, the words of God's prophets, her head crowned with twelve stars, the authority of the twelve apostles of Christ.

The revelator says further, "And there appeared another wonder in heaven; and behold a great red dragon, having seven heads and ten horns, and seven crowns upon his heads" (Revelation 12:3). The woman not being literal, could this great dragon be a literal beast? Remember, we are commanded to compare "spiritual things with spiritual" (1 Corinthians 2:13).

Before concluding who this dragon is, let us read more of the prophecy: "And she brought forth a man child, who was to rule all nations with a rod of iron" (Revelation 12:4). This man-child represents Christ and His saints, all children of the true wisdom of God.

When these faithful children are born into immortal life at the coming of Jesus, this man-child will have been born. Christ, the head of this man-child who is to rule the world in righteousness, was born into immortality more than 1,900 years ago. But as Paul declares, "Every man in his own order: Christ the first fruits; afterward they that are Christ's at his coming" (1 Corinthians 15:23). All others must wait until His second coming.

At this time, according to the revelator's vision, when the man-child received authority, there was war in heaven: "Michael and his angels fought against the dragon; and the dragon fought and his angels, and prevailed not; neither was their place found any more in heaven. And the great dragon was cast out, that old serpent, called the Devil, and Satan, which deceiveth the whole world: he was cast out into the earth, and his angels were cast out with him" (Revelation 12:7–9). This great dragon is representative of all forms of evil extant upon earth at Christ's return. It is the same devil and Satan who have been working down through the ages—sin, darkness and iniquity, and all those who promote them.

Taking place in heaven, this war is a battle between the leaders of the darkness of this world and Christ and His saints; its location is the political heavens, the seat of authority. And who shall prevail in this great battle, this war in heaven? Christ and His saints, for the "great dragon was cast out, that old serpent, called the Devil, and Satan." All evil will be suppressed down to earth, though not destroyed until the end of the millennial reign.

The Devil Bound, Loosed, Destroyed

During the glorious, thousand-year day—the millennial reign of Christ—the devil (evil) will be bound. Revelation 20:1–3 is unambiguous: "And I saw an angel come down from heaven, having the key of the bottomless pit and a great chain in his hand. And he laid hold on the dragon, that old serpent, which is the Devil, and Satan, and bound him a thousand years, and cast him into the bottomless pit, and shut him up, and set a seal upon him, that he should deceive the nations no more, till the thousand years should be fulfilled: and after that he must be loosed a little season." Certainly this description could not be taken literally; how could a spiritual pit confine a literal devil?

During the thousand years, evil will be bound in the hearts of men; they will not dare openly disobey the law of God, as so many do now. Another divine forecast applies to this period: "And thine ears shall hear a word behind thee, saying, This is the way, walk ye in it, when ye turn to the right hand, and when ye turn to the left" (Isaiah 30:21).

At the end of the thousand years, Satan shall "be loosed a little season," after which he shall be cast into the "lake of fire," "which is the second death" (Revelation 20:14 and 10; 21:8). Sin and evil shall perish forever from the earth, and nothing but righteousness and holiness, peace and love, will survive to bless with pleasures forevermore the immortal inhabitants of an earth made new. Far from interfering in that heavenly new world, the devil shall belong to the "former" which "shall not be remembered, nor come into mind" (Isaiah 65:17).

Regarding the concept of a supernatural devil, I have argued that there is no such creature. The devil of popular belief does not exist as a personal devil fallen from heaven. However, several scriptures point toward a real supernatural devil or Satan.

As I have already explained, the words *Satan* and *devil* can both be defined as "adversary" or "accuser." An adversary exists—a devil—who will bring harm and death to people who disobey the Lord's will. Let's look at several scriptural examples of disobedience, and determine who is the adversary or devil in each situation.

Example 1:

After Adam and Eve disobeyed God, they were sentenced to return to the ground. God condemned Adam to death. "In the sweat of thy face shalt thou eat bread, till thou return unto the ground" (Genesis 3:19). If Satan had the power of death, why did He not kill Adam and Eve while they were in the garden?

Because of Moses's sin of disobedience, He was prohibited from entering the Promised Land and condemned to die. "And the Lord spoke unto Moses that self same day, saying, 'Get thee up into this mountain Abarim ... And die on the Mount whether thou goest up ... because ye trespassed against me among the children of Israel at the waters of Meribah-Kadesh'" (Deuteronomy 32:48–51). Why did God kill Moses? It was because He disobeyed God. It was not a personal devil that demanded his death, but God himself.

The Killing of Aaron

Aaron shall be gathered unto his people, for he shall not enter into the land which I have given unto the children of Israel, because ye rebelled against my word at the waters of Meribah. Take Aaron and Eleazar his son, and bring them up unto mount Hor; and strip Aaron of his garments and put them upon Eleazar his son. And Aaron shall be gathered unto his people, and shall die there ... And Moses stripped Aaron of his garments, and put them upon Eleazar his son, and Aaron died there on the top of the mount: and Moses and Eleazar came down from the mount. (Numbers 20:24–28)

All of this was caused by an act of disobedience to God's word at Meribah. Disobedience to God will get you killed. Nothing is mentioned of a supernatural Satan that was cast out of heaven. There's no fallen angel here, only God.

Example 2:

Another example is found in 1 Samuel. Uzzah was close to the ark, which was on a new cart. When they came to Nachon's threshing floor, Uzzah put forth his hand to the ark of God and took hold of it, for the oxen shook it. "And the anger of the Lord was kindled against Uzzah, and God smote him there for his error [sin] and there he died by the ark of God" (1 Samuel 6:7). No one was supposed to touch the ark, so Uzzah's disobedience got him killed. Who killed Uzzah? God did. Why? Because Uzzah had disobeyed God. It is better to obey than to fast forty days.

Example 3:

Another sin of disobedience is found in 1 Kings: "And behold, there came a man of God out of Judah by the word of the Lord" (13:1). The Lord told this man neither to eat and drink nor to turn back, but He disobeyed the Lord's words. The man of God ate and drank, and then "he saddled his ass to wit and … when he was gone a Lion met him by the way and slew him by the way and his carcass was cast in the way" (1 Kings 13:23–24). Notice the statement in verse 26. The man of God was disobedient unto the word of the Lord. Disobedience is sin, and it carries the death sentence. This scriptural passage says nothing about a supernatural being called Satan sent to kill the man of God, but only about God sending a lion.

2 Peter 2:4

In 2 Peter 2:4, we read, "For if God spare not the angels that sinned, but cast them down to hell, and delivered them into chains of darkness, to be reserved unto judgment." Who are these angels that were cast down to hell, which are in the grave and bound in chains of darkness, waiting on the judgment? This is what happens to all who die and are buried. You are in a deep hole in the ground, waiting on the judgment day. The body returns to the ground and the spirit to the father.

This passage is found in the book of Jude: "And the angels which kept not their first estate, but left their own habitation, he hath reserved in everlasting chains under darkness unto the judgment of the great day" (v. 6). Jude said these angels were cast down to hell because they kept not their first estate, but left their own habitation. The term *estate* refers to where they lived and their position or rank, such as pastor, priest, or leader in the church—called angels of the Lord or messengers.

Angels are considered God's leaders on earth and in heaven, charged as chiefs or high priests to get the message to the people. Jude tells us that these angels were the people who came out of the land of Egypt. "The Lord, having saved the people out of the land of Egypt, destroyed them that believed not" (Jude v. 5).

— Is This Proof of a Supernatural Devil? —

In this passage, the seven stars are the angels of the seven churches, and the seven candlesticks are the seven churches: "The mystery of the seven stars which thou sawest in my right hand, and the seven golden candlesticks" (Revelation 1:20). These angels were priests of God, flesh and blood humans, as we can see in the seven churches of this first chapter of Revelation. "Saying, I am Alpha and Omega, the first and the last ... and what thou seest, write in a book, and send it unto the seven churches: unto Ephesus, and unto Smyrna, and unto Pergamos, and unto Thyatira, and unto Sardis, and unto Philadelphia, and unto Laodicea" (Revelation 1:8 and 11).

Seven churches, represented as candlesticks, are on the seven hills, and each church had a priest to minister to the people at Passover and make offering for the people. These priests are called *stars* in Revelation 1:20, and each church has a male priest:

- "Unto the angel [priest] of the church of Ephesus write ..." (2:1)

- "And unto the angel [priest] of the church in Smyrna write ..." (2:8)
- "And unto the angel [priest] of the church in Pergamos write ..." (2:12)
- "And unto the angel [priest] of the church in Thyatira write ..." (2:18)
- "And unto the angel [priest] of the church in Sardis write ..." (3:1)
- "And to the angel [priest] of the church in Philadelphia write ..." (3:7)
- "And unto the angel [priest] of the church of the Laodiceans write ..." (3:14)

This has nothing to do with seven church ages that represent seven periods of times before the return of Christ. This was a message to the churches of that day and time, which no longer exist. We can, however, learn from these churches from a historical point of view. Again the church makes assumptions, and they hold on to their theological doctrine.

The angels of all these churches mentioned in Revelation were priests or pastors, flesh-and-blood people. So we see that angels can be humans who work for the Lord, just like the leaders under Moses who were killed for leaving their first estate.

Did angels marry women, engage in sex, and have children? In Luke 24:39, Jesus said, "Behold my hands and my feet, that it is I myself: handle me, and see, for a spirit hath not flesh and bones, as ye see me have." Jesus said He had flesh and bone, but He doesn't mention having blood, because His blood was drained on the cross.

Jesus said "a spirit hath not flesh and bones," but we read this in Hebrews 1:7: "And of the angels he saith, who maketh his angels spirits, and his ministers a flame of fire." The Word said God's angels are spirits, and Jesus said they don't have flesh and bone. If the angels don't have flesh, how can they have sex and produce a human baby?

Paul was repeating Psalm 104:4, and in Romans 8:14, we read, "For as many as are led by the Spirit of God, they are the sons of God." These are humans on earth and not in heaven, but they are sons of God.

We read in Galatians 4:6, "And because ye are sons," and again in 1 John 3:1, "Behold, what manner of love the father hath bestowed upon us, that we should be called the sons of God." First John 3:2 tells us, "Beloved, now are we the sons of God." Angels are messengers, whether spirit or flesh, and they do not have the ability to reproduce. If angels could reproduce, there would be no need for people to reproduce to fill the kingdom.

Some people argue that angels had sex with women, who then gave birth to hybrid children who grew into giants, but this is not found in the Word of God. According to Hebrews 2:7, "Thou madest him a little lower than the angels" Jesus said of himself in John 5:19, "Most assuredly, I say to you, the son can do nothing of himself." If Jesus could do nothing of himself, being made lower than the angels, how could an angel do more? The angels would have a standard higher than a man of flesh and blood.

Jesus said, "For I have come down from heaven, not to do my own will, but the will of him who sent me" (John 6:38). So did God create angels with the ability to do good and evil in heaven and to comment fornication at will? If such activity happens in heaven, why should we pray for God's will to be done on earth as it is in heaven? If evil exists in heaven and angels can do whatever they want to is God in control or not? If angels from heaven had sex with women, what is there to stop this from happening again, even today?

If sons of God in heaven and on earth are doing evil of the same nature, why would we need a new heaven and a new earth? I understand God is in the heavens above, which is a paradise to hope for. I believe the angels created by God are perfect, and they come and go by God's command to accomplish His will. And I believe that the angels want to do God's will, just as Jesus said, "Not my will, but thine be done" (Luke 22:42).

"There were Nephilim [giants] in the earth in those days and also after that, when the Sons of God came in unto the daughters of men, and they bear children to them, the same became mighty men which were of old, men of renown" (Genesis 6:4). These men took wives and had children, but there is nothing to suggest that these sons of God were angels. Genesis says these men were sons of God, men of old, and men of renown.

Renown can be defined as a state of being widely acclaimed and highly honored. A person of renown is a notable person with a popular reputation. These men of renown were looked up to and respected, men of good report who were highly respected by those around them.

"Men of old" would be people whom we think of as our seniors, men of a generation or two before us. We use the phrase *old man* to refer to a father, a husband, or a commanding officer. This event took place before Noah built the ark, so these men were older than Noah. We can find the answer in God's holy Word. We must look for old men, before Noah, who were respected and had a good report (Genesis 5:1–32).

Good men	Not-so-good men
Adam	Cain
Eve	Irad, the son of Enoch 365
Seth	Mehujael
Enos	Methusael 969
Cainan	Jabel
Mahalaleel	Jubal
Jared	tubal-Cain
Methuselah	Arphaxad
Lamech	Sem
Noah	

These are men of renown and men who disobeyed the Lord with their families.

The sons and daughters did not start to multiply until the birth of Seth, Enos, and Enoch. Their families were larger with sons and daughters. We see the men of old, as young as 365 years and as old as 969 years. These men were the men of renown, respected and looked up to.

But the Bible says they were the sons of God. Yes, it does. The term *sons of God* do not always refer to God himself, but also to His sons and their sons. Luke 3:23–38 begins with Joseph, the son of Heli, and continues through Adam as the son of God. Jesus takes us from His day backward through the family tree of Joseph's father, Heli, through Adam, the father of Seth.

In the Genesis account (Genesis 6:2), the sons of God saw that the daughters of men were fair, and they took them as wives. Again, nothing is said of angels of a supernatural origin becoming flesh and cohabiting with the daughters of men, only that they were renowned men of old with a good report.

The men listed above are the sons and grandsons of Adam. Luke 3:38

is the key: "Which was the son of Enos, which was the son of Seth, which was the son of Adam, which was the son of God." Adam and his entire family were sons of God! Both the righteous and the unrighteous, the good and the evil, were sons of God. The sons of God were Adam's sons and grandsons. Angels didn't add to the problems that caused God to destroy the earth. The existence of giants in the land does not mean they were the children of angels.

Human Beings as Angels

"And he hath slandered thy servant unto my Lord the King, but my Lord, the King David is as an angel of God: do therefore what is good in thine eyes" (2 Samuel 19:27). In this case, the king was an angel, which brings us back to the question of angels in the writings of Peter and Jude. They were having problems with other ministers in the area who were preaching and teaching things that were not true. Those ministers were teaching from the *Book of Enoch* and other sources, which tried to place blame on the heavenly angel of God rather than on the earthly angels—priests and other leaders in high positions, such as Moses.

What Angels Were Peter and Jude Talking About?

In 2 Peter 2:4, he did not say these angels were cast from heaven to hell, but only that they were cast down to hell to be reserved until the day of judgment. The angels or leaders in high positions who were cast down to hell were the leaders who opposed Moses in the wilderness. "I will therefore put you in remembrance, though ye once knew this, how that the Lord, having saved the people out of the land of Egypt, afterward destroyed them that believed not" (Jude v. 5).

Numbers 16:1–3

In the following passage from Numbers, these men believed they also were holy sons of God like Moses. Adam was a son of God, and they were his descendants:

> Now Korah, the son of Izhar, the son of Kohath, the son of Levi, and Dathan and Abiram, the son of Eliab, and On, the son of Peleth, sons of Reuben took *men*. And they rose up before Moses, with certain of the children of Israel, two hundred and fifty princes [angels] of the assembly, famous in the congregation, men of renown [highly respected of old]. And they gathered themselves together against Moses and against Aaron, and said unto them, ye take too much upon you, seeing that the entire congregations are holy, every one of them, and the Lord is among them: wherefore then lift ye up yourselves above the congregation of the Lord? (Numbers 16:1–3)

These leaders and the 250 princes all agreed that Moses took the lead and always had the final say in what the house of Israel did. They desired to return to Egypt, but Moses and Aaron said, "No, we are waiting on the Lord to lead us." The leaders in the camp did not like this. So they took a stand against Moses, left the priesthood, and stopped serving. These were men of God, chosen as leaders of the tribe of Israel to be priests and servants, messengers and angels under Moses's leadership—and they refused to work in the temple.

Numbers 16:8–9

"And Moses said unto Korah, hear, I pray you, ye sons of Levi: Seemeth it but a small thing unto you that the God of Israel hath separated you from the congregation of Israel, to bring you near to himself to do the service of the tabernacle of the Lord, and stand before the congregation to minister unto them?" (Numbers 16:8–9). They took their jobs lightly.

In verse 6 of Jude, we read that these angels (priests) had left their first estate (positions as priests) and moved from the tabernacle where they had lived. In Numbers 16:9, we read that the priests removed themselves from the tabernacle and did not minister to the congregation. Because they left their positions as ministers—their first estate, as recorded in Jude—God separated them from the congregation. Moses tried to get these leaders and priests to return and do the job of ministering to their congregations as before, but they all refused.

Numbers 16:12

"And Moses sent to call Dathan and Abiram, the sons of Eliab, which said, 'We will not come up'" (Numbers 16:12). These men were chosen to serve in the tabernacle and minister to the people, and they made it clear that they were rebelling against God, not Moses. All they could see was the wilderness, without the milk and honey that had been promised, so they stopped working as ministers of God. They had been the angels, leaders, or stars of the camp of Israel.

The Lord told Moses to separate from this group, so Moses and the elders went to the tabernacle of Korah and Dathan and told Abiram to separate themselves from the congregation. The Lord was going to destroy all these people, because they had become His adversaries.

Numbers 16:26

While Moses, Aaron, and the elders were leaving Korah, Dathan, and Abiram's tabernacle, Moses spoke these words to them as they stood in the door of their tents: "Depart, I pray you, from the tents of these wicked men [angels or leaders], and touch nothing of theirs, lest ye be consumed in all their sins" (Numbers 16:26). (Wicked men were also known as a Satan or devils, as adversaries.) Their wives, sons, and little children were with them, listening to what Moses had to say. The mothers were concerned about their children, knowing what had happened in the past when Moses spoke. Their husbands had been excommunicated from the camp.

Numbers 16:28

"And Moses said, hereby ye shall know that the Lord hath sent me to do all these works; for I have not done them of mine own mind" (Numbers 16:28). In other words, they would learn shortly about their mistake. Jude and Peter said these angels or messengers of God were cast down to hell—not from heaven, but cast down to hell—after Moses finished talking about what was about to happen because these men had provoked the Lord and left their first estate. These were angels or messengers who refused to do what the Lord required, thus becoming fallen angels or ministers of God here on earth.

The reason of reviewing these events is to explain them in more detail, so that we can more easily understand the word as it applies to the subject.

Numbers 16:31

As soon as Moses stopped talking, "It came to pass, as he had made an end of speaking all these words, that the ground clave asunder that was under them. And the earth opened her mouth, and swallowed them up, and their houses, and all the men that appertained unto Korah, and all their goods" (Numbers 16:31–32). These angels or messengers are angels in the same respect as the angels of Revelation 3:1. Priests and pastors are messengers, angels of God. "And unto the angel of the church in Sardis write ..." (Revelation 1:20). The angel mentioned here is the pastor of the Sardis church—a human, not a supernatural being.

"They, and all that appertained to them, went down alive into the pit, and the earth closed upon them: and they perished from them among the congregation" (Numbers 16:33). Remember that in 2 Peter 2:4 and Jude v. 6, these angels or tribe leaders were cast down to hell (the grave)? Isn't this what happens in Numbers 16:33? The pit was the grave!

The congregation stood by and watched what God did, and heard all the men, women, children, and animals all crying. Then the people ran away, fearing they also might be destroyed. These leaders with Korah were all buried alive and the earth closed over them, covering them up along with their livestock. During this time, the 250 priests (angels) were doing their job, but they were part of the Korah group, bound in darkness (the grave) until the judgment.

Numbers 16:35

"And there came out a fire from the Lord and consumed the two hundred and fifty men that offered incense" (Numbers 16:35). These priests (angels) were burned alive, worshipping at the altar. The very next day the people came to Moses, complained about what had happened, and started a riot against Moses and Aaron. The Lord told Moses to get out of the way, so that He could destroy the people. Moses went on his face before the Lord, but that did not stop the Lord from sending His wrath.

God started killing people, and Moses had to act fast to stop it. "And Moses said unto Aaron, 'Take a sensor [a fire pan], and put fire therein from off the altar, and put on incense, and go quickly unto the congregation, and make atonement for them: for there is wrath gone out from the Lord; the plague is begun'" (Numbers 16:46).

Before the plague was stopped, it had killed 14,700 people. This happened before Aaron could get the fire pan and incense together and position himself between the congregation and grave site of those buried alive. What a sight to see! It is God who is doing the killing.

Numbers 16:49

"Now they that died in the plague were fourteen thousand and seven hundred, besides them that died about the matter of Korah" (Numbers 16:49). In two days, Korah and all his people with their livestock were killed or buried alive by the Lord, and 250 priests (angels) who were offering incense were set afire and burned alive. About 15,000 went to hell, plus 250 burned alive! Peter and Jude tell us they were cast down quickly, which is how it is described in Numbers 16:30 "And they go down quick into the pit." There they remain until the judgment, in chains of darkness.

Peter and Jude recorded this event, not a story about heavenly angels as in the book of Enoch. They knew that the teaching of the Book of

Enoch was in error. These angels were not cast out of heaven, but down into earth quickly. All we have about these angels is in Peter and Jude, who don't tell us that the angels were ever in heaven or engaged in destroying people on earth.

This is all the information we have on the subject, and it is scanty and obscure. It does not tell of angels being expelled from heaven to engage in barbarous expeditions against human interest and divine authority, wherever their caprice might lead them. It does, however, tell us about the disobedience of angels, not necessarily in heaven, who were then confirmed in the grave against a time of judgment. It speaks of them as in custody, "under chains of darkness," expressing the bondage of death in which they are held and from which they will emerge, to be judged, when the saints shall sit in judgment. Paul asks in 1 Corinthians 6:3, "Know ye not that we shall judge angels?" The time of their fall and location are matters of speculation, but the leaders of the twelve tribes will judge them.

Many churches and ministers quote Revelation 12 as proof of how Satan arrived on earth in the beginning. "And there was war in heaven: Michael and his Angels fought against the dragon and the dragon fought and his Angels, and prevailed not, neither was their place found anymore in heaven. And the dragon was cast out, that old serpent called the Devil, and Satan, which deceiveth the whole world: he was cast out unto the earth, and his angels were cast out with him" (Revelation 12:7–9). What heaven are we talking about, the heaven where God himself lives or the heavens of high places as recorded in the Bible, where spiritual wickedness reigns?

Was the Rebellion in Heaven Before Adam?

John writes in Revelation 1:1, "The Revelation of Jesus Christ, which God gave unto him [Jesus], to shew unto his servant's things which must shortly come to pass, and he sent and signified it by his angel unto his servant John." God revealed to Jesus—and the angel told John—about things that would happen at a later day but not too far off. Two thousand years later is not a short time from a human perspective, but to God it is.

The things John saw in Revelation were representative of events yet to happen in the future, not before the creation of Adam and Eve. Yet many people interpret the book as though it describes events that happened before John's day, and even as early as the creation of the world and the so-called war between God and Satan that destroyed the first earth. How plain can it be, that everything John saw would come to pass after his vision or sleep on the Lord's Day? (See Revelation 1.1 and 4:2.)

When Will Satan Be Cast Out of Heaven? Was He Ever in Heaven?

"After this I looked, and behold, a door was opened in heaven: and the first voice which I heard was as it were of a trumpet talking with me; which said, 'Come up hither, and I will shew thee things which must be *hereafter*'" (Revelation 4:1). How can we incorrectly place the war and casting out of Satan from heaven to earth *before* Adam's day? God said to Jesus, the angel, and John that these events would happen "hereafter." Remember, John was passed out in the Spirit (Revelation 1:10).

What John saw were not actual things, but signs and symbols of real things. The proof is in Revelation 1:1: "Jesus … sent and signified it by his angel unto his servant John." All the things John saw were symbols and representative of things that are real.

Taking a Look at Some Symbols

(1) The seven churches of Asia are represented by seven candlesticks (Revelation 1:12). John tells us, "I saw seven golden candlesticks" (Revelation 1:12). These candlesticks represent the angels, priests, or pastors—the leaders of the seven churches. In verse 20, we read, "and the seven candlesticks which thou sawest are the seven churches." The priests or leaders of these churches were recognized as angels. The seven candlesticks symbolize actual churches in Asia that existed at the time of John and the future churches with their shortcoming of the gospel.

(2) A seven-horned lamb symbolizes Christ (Revelation 5:6).

(3) A woman symbolizes a city. In Revelation 12:1, we read, "And there

appeared a great wonder in heaven, a woman clothed with the sun, and the moon under her feet, and upon her head a crown of twelve stars" She is opposed by a dragon with seven heads and ten horns, who, with his tail, sweeps the third part of the stars from their places in the sky.

— When Was Satan Cast Out of Heaven? —

When was Satan cast out of heaven, and from which heaven was he cast out? Was it the heaven of Luke 10:18? In Hebrew (Chaldean), heaven is *Shamayin*.[8] This heaven is no higher than the clouds, as described in Ephesians: "the Prince and power of the air" (1:2).

In the Strong's Concordance the Greek word *ouranos*,[9] translated into English, never meant the heaven where God is, but can mean heights or high places. In Luke's Gospel, where we read, "I saw Satan fall as lightning from heaven," most scholars would say "from high places." Jesus didn't mean that Satan was with God, but only that Satan was falling from high places (as in world systems).

In Ephesians 6:12, Paul said, "against principalities, against powers, against the rulers of the darkness of this world, against spiritual wickedness in high places." We could accurately replace "high places" with "heavenly places," but that doesn't refer to the heaven where God exists. We see this wickedness today in all of our world systems; none are exempted. People who say that there are no supernatural beings around us are wrong, but that doesn't mean there is a supernatural personal devil who fell from the grace of God and is bent on destroying everything God stands for.

— The Book of Revelation —

The book of Revelation is believed by some scholars to have been written around 95 AD, although others believe it was written much earlier. Revelation wasn't included in the Bible until 397 AD, when the Counsel of

---

[8] Cruden 8065.
[9] Strong 3771.

Carthage decided to add it. In 70 AD, the City of Jerusalem was destroyed and its books were burned. Much of what we have today was found among the ruins of the city, or it was buried and then discovered at a much later date. The religious systems were already established and married to Rome, the ruling state.

Revelation was not included in the religious texts of second-century Christians of Syria. It was written during their great tribulation at the hands of Nero and others. Revelation is considered a heretic book by orthodox churches.

Revelation 12:7–12

Some people believe that Revelation 12:7–12 proves that a supernatural being called Satan does exist, but does it?

> And there was war in heaven: Michael and his angels fought against the dragon; and the dragon fought and his angels, and prevailed not; neither was their place found anymore in heaven. And the great dragon was cast out, that old serpent called the Devil, and Satan, which deceiveth the whole world: he was cast out into the earth, and his angels were cast out with him. And I heard a loud voice saying in heaven, "Now is come salvation, and strength, and the kingdom of our God, and the power of his Christ: for the accuser of our brethren is cast down, which accused them before our God day and night." (Revelation 12:7–10)

Notice the word *accuser*, which is how *Satan* is defined in *Strong's Concordance*.

"And they overcame him by the blood of the Lamb and by the word of their testimony; and they loved not their lives unto death" (Revelation 12:11). Could this be the same as sin being cast down by the death of Christ? Could this be the war—Christ conquering the devil, or sin, for our salvation?

"Therefore rejoice ye heavens, and ye that dwell in them. Woe to the inhabiters of the earth and of the sea! For the Devil is come down unto you, having great wrath, because he knoweth that he hath but a short time" (Revelation 12:12). Was John talking about Nero having a short time to live? This is the scripture that many churches believe supports the theory of a real supernatural devil. At the time of this writing, John was living a life of depression caused by the world system under Nero's leadership.

Which heaven are we talking about? Is it the heaven where God lives? The third heaven or the heaven called Shamayin (Hebrew) or ouranos (Greek)? God is in neither place. The war could have been in high places, such as the church and state of their day.

Is there any scriptural proof that a Satan was ever in heaven? Surely God controls His house. We would like to believe that the Lord would surely not let a devil live in the same house with him, especially a devil that will try to destroy what God has in heaven.

When rulers of countries lose their fights to remain in power, we say that they are "cast down," meaning they have lost their position in the system. It does not mean they were "cast down" from the heaven inhabited by God. Sin cannot approach God in heaven. How can God's house be entered by evil, such as a Satan who is trying to destroy God's kingdom? That can never happen.

Remember the people of Moses who were killed? I said that those leaders were called angels, even though they were human. Can I prove this? Remember that those angels of the church are priests of God—human, not spirits. The angel of the Lord tells John in Revelation 2:12, "And to the angel [priest] of the church in Pergamos write; 'These things saith he which hath the sharp sword [word] with two edges." In Revelation 2:13, we read, "I know thy works and where thou dwellest, even where Satan's seat is."

The Lord's angel said he knew where Satan's seat was and where he lived. This angel was a ruler here on earth that lived in Pergamos and had many Christians killed, including a servant or minister by the name of Antipas, a faithful individual who was slain by this devil. The serpent, Satan, the devil that killed Antipas was human, a flesh-and-blood person. Antipas, a bishop in Pergamos was told to deny his Christian faith, but he refused to deny Jesus as Lord. He was placed inside a bull, like Vat on the altar of Zeus, and boiled alive for his faith—a martyr.

Who was this devil? He was the brother of Litus Flavius, who destroyed Jerusalem in 70 AD. He and his brother were of the empire of Rome and of the German race. The Satan that called himself "Master and God" was the Roman emperor Domitiare in 92 AD. He was cast down, as the vision said, killed by the sword of his own court. Jesus said in Luke 10:18, "I beheld Satan as lightning fall from heaven." Jesus saw Satan fall, the same way He saw Jerusalem fall in 70 AD. We can see from this that, thus far, there are no supernatural devils or angels fallen from God's heaven.

Revelation 1:9

John said he was in tribulation, just like all others who believe in Christ: "I, John, who also am your brother, and companion in tribulation, and in the kingdom and patience of Jesus Christ, was in the isle that is called Patmos, for the word of God, and for the testimony of Jesus Christ. I was in the spirit on the Lord's Day, and heard behind me a great voice, as of a trumpet" (Revelation 1:9–10).

Nothing that John saw, including what is described in Revelation 12:7–12, happened in Noah's day—as believed by people who try to prove that this war was in heaven before the flood, and that the angels married and had babies who became giants. This cannot be true.

Revelation 1:1

"The revelation of Jesus Christ, which God gave unto him, to show unto his servants things which must shortly come to pass; and he sent and signified it by his angel unto his servant John" (Revelation 1:1). The angel told John that this was "things which must shortly come to pass," so this could not be a war before and during Noah's day. All the powers of the Roman empire began to fall, including the religious system of the day that had remained from the day of Moses, with its high priest in 70 AD.

Revelation 12 Tells a Story of Two Wonders that John Saw in Heaven

(1) The first wonder is about a woman clothed with the sun, with the moon under her feet and a crown of twelve stars on her head, and ready to be delivered of a child.

(2) The second wonder is a great red dragon with seven heads and ten horns, and a tail that swept away a third of the stars of heaven.

This is not the heaven where God lives, and it contains no reference to Satan being cast out of heaven. The church world, in its teachings on this subject, is making assumptions that this proves the dragon is, in fact, Satan the devil cast down and pulling a third of God's angels with him from heaven. If God couldn't save His angels from Satan, what chance do we have of being protected?

The great red dragon could only be a ruler with seven assistants, symbolized by the seven heads. The ten horns symbolize the powers of the system that, when it fell, meant the fall of a third of his kingdom. This dragon fell not from heaven where God is, but from the heaven of high places in earth's systems. We can see the same thing taking place today around the world.

1. The woman was on earth with child ready to be delivered. Could this represent the church today, or the recording of the birth of Jesus in difficult times?
2. The dragon was on earth with the woman ready to kill her child. Could this be Herod?
3. The woman had a man-child who was caught up to God—a single child, not a group of Christians flying away to heaven. Could the man-child represent Christ?
4. The woman fled to the wilderness, not to heaven. This is what John saw, in the spirit in heaven that was to take place shortly: "Come up hither, and I will shew thee things which must be hereafter" (Revelation 4:1). Things "hereafter" are things he saw that would be "after" him, later. This probably doesn't mean 1,900 years later, but it could refer to 70 AD or 95 AD.

Everything in chapter 12 took place on earth, so it does not support the concept of a supernatural devil cast out of heaven, as some believe. Verse 11 proves that it was on earth: "And they overcame him [the dragon] by the blood of the Lamb, and by the word of their testimony, and they loved not their lives unto the death" (Revelation 12:11). The blood of Jesus was shed on earth, not in heaven, and many believers were killed for their belief. There is no death in heaven, and this chapter does not prove the existence of a supernatural being.

In John's vision, he saw a corrupt religious system and its rulers who persecuted Christians from the very beginning of the church. The religious system was about to be brought down, and it did fall in 70 AD. Most of their problems were with the Edomite priesthood in that day. The priests then were much like the priests of today; they believe themselves to be gods on earth.

Revelation 12:1–17 does not prove that a supernatural being was cast out of God's heaven. It was only a vision of what was to happen shortly after John's time. The dragon is overcome the same way today as in John's day, by the blood and our testimony in Christ.

The King of Tyrus

Ezekiel 28:12–15

This passage in Ezekiel is used by some Christians to prove that this king of Tyrus represented Satan. We will investigate this king and see if, in fact, he is Satan. We will also investigate the nature of the prince.

Who Is the Prince?

What seems to prove this prince to be Satan or his representative? The church of the Christian community preaches, teaches, and believes this to be Satan, a supernatural fallen angel, cast out of heaven, but is that true?

In Ezekiel 28, what would cause anyone to believe this to be Satan? Here are several positive things that might suggest that to be true, from the first two verses:

1. He is a prince.
2. His heart is lifted up.
3. He says he is a god.
4. He says that he is seated in the seat of a god.
5. He is in the midst of the seas.
6. He is wiser than Daniel; no secret can be hid from him.

Now let's look at some negative aspects of this prince:

1. He is a prince with a warning from the Lord of Hosts.
2. His heart is lifted up with pride, which would indicate a heart of flesh.
3. He was rebuked by the Lord God because he said he was a god.
4. He sits in the seat of a god as a god.
5. God says that he is a man, not a god; he only thinks he is a god.
6. He is good at making money through trade and commerce at the seaport in Tyrus.

God said because the prince's heart is defiled, he will be brought down to the pit (grave). His heart—his thinking and intent—are evil. The prince is just a man, and he shall die with those slain in the seas. Can Satan die?

The Lord asks him, in verse 9, "What will you say to the person that will kill you." How could a supernatural being, be killed by a mere human? Yet Satan is to be killed by a person of human nature. He was a devil to the people of that day—a human devil, not a supernatural being.

The word of the Lord is clear on this matter: the prince was a man, a human being, who would be killed, just as the Lord said. He was neither a god nor a supernatural being cast down from heaven. The problem was not with the prince, however, but with the king of Tyrus. The king of Tyrus was said to be a supernatural being, Satan, but was he?

The King of Tyrus

At the time of this king, the city of Tyrus (or Tyre) was a rich Phoenician seaport, which is called Lebanon today. Where did the church get the idea that the king of Tyrus was Satan?

Ezekiel 27:2 says, "Now, thou son of man, take up a lamentation for Tyrus." This message is a warning for the whole city of Tyrus, not just the prince and king. The people of Tyrus and their city council bragged and praised themselves for all their accomplishments and their good lives.

During this time, Ithobaal (or Ithobalus) was king of Tyrus. He had a god called Melkart, whose temple had a garden. Most temples had gardens, like those of Solomon and Nebuchadnezzar. God met and talked with Adam and Eve in the Garden of Eden. In our larger cities today, we refer to such gardens as parks.

In their interpretation of Ezekiel 28:12–20, many churches and Bible scholars view the king of Tyrus as a supernatural being. Why would they do that? The church and its followers must have a Satan or devil, but why? Because. They need something that they can blame all their problems on. It is no fun to admit our own shortcomings and problems. So here is why the church believes the king of Tyrus to be Satan:

1. He was wise and perfect in beauty. (Verse 12)
2. He had been in Eden, the garden of God. (Verse 13) (Many people lived in Eden during this time.)
3. He was covered with precious stones. (Verse 13)
4. He was the anointed cherub (protector or instrument) that covereth, and God made it so. (Verse 14)
5. He was upon the holy mountain of God. (Verse 14)
6. He walked up and down the stones of fire. (Verse 14)

This king had a good thing going. The church believes he was Satan because he was perfect, in Eden, covered with precious stones, and—most of all—an anointed cherub. The church believes these features prove that the king of Tyrus was Satan, a supernatural being. If this is true, the church should rejoice and be glad it was. As we will see later, a cherub is not an angel. Adam was the only one in the garden who was perfect. The serpent was already a rebel, a devil waiting for the right time to bring down Adam.

The Six Things Listed: Do They Prove the King of Tyrus Was a Supernatural Being?

1. Ithobaal III was king in 573 BC, at the time of Ezekiel 28. He was smart and wise, but that does not make him a supernatural being. Solomon was wise and rich, too, but he wasn't supernatural.
2. Being in God's Garden of Eden does not make King Ithobaal a supernatural being. As explained above, the Garden of Eden was a park in which to walk around and relax.

The house of Eden (Bit-Adini) Beth-Eden was a city and a place where God had a garden, and it did exist in the time of this king. Eden was in Arabia. Adam and Eve were evicted out of the garden (park) by God, but the place still exists. God did not destroy Eden. Eden was a place with a garden in it (Ben e'edhem). It is known as Avan and Beth-Aven, which means a place where God had a garden. It can be found in the maps section of most Bibles today.

Ezekiel 27:23

"Haran, and Canneh, and "EDEN," the merchants of Sheba, Asshur, and Chilmad, were thy merchants." The Eden people were trading with the king of Tyrus?

Amos 1:5

"I will break also the bar of Damascus, and cut off the inhabitant from the plain of Aven, and him that holdeth the sceptre from the house of Eden; and the people of Syria shall go into captivity unto Kir, saith the Lord"

(Amos 1:5). *Webster's Ninth New Collegiate Dictionary* defines *sceptre* as "one who holds the authority."[10] Like the White House in Washington, DC, holds the authority? In the Bible we find that the scepter was held by the tribe of Judah, from which Jesus came. And one day He will take the position of leader of the world and hold the scepter Himself.

Hosea 4:15

"Though thou, Israel, played the harlot, yet let not Judah offend; and come not ye unto Gilgal, neither go ye up to Beth-Aven, nor swear, The Lord liveth" (Amos 4:15). Beth-Aven was the place where God had a garden known as the Garden of Eden.

Note: During the time of this king, Daniel, Isaiah, Hosea, Joel, Amos, Hezekiah, the three Hebrew boys, and Nebuchadnezzar were all living.

In Amos 1:9, the house of Eden went into captivity, and in Isaiah 37:12 we find that the city of Eden was destroyed. "Have the gods of the nations delivered them which my fathers have destroyed, as Gozan, and Haran, and Rezeph, and the children of Eden, which were in Telassar?" (Isaiah 37:12). These places are all in the Mesopotamia area.

Eden existed and was conquered in 856 BC, during the reign of the king of Tyrus (2 Kings 19:12). Living in Eden did not mean that the king was supernatural; there was a whole city of people in Eden and Aven where God had a garden (Bit-Adini) Eden east of Bethel, and the king could have lived there at some time.

―――――――――――― **Precious Stones** ――――――――――――

What need would a supernatural devil or heavenly being have for precious stones here on earth, unless he were human? I do not know of any angels wearing precious stones. But what king in those days didn't dress up with all types of gold, silver, and precious stones? Kings did so to proudly show their glory and riches in pride. This did not make a king supernatural or a

10 *Webster's Ninth New Collegiate Dictionary*, s.v. "sceptre."

Satan cast down out of heaven. Angels have no need for earthly things to show off. Only a person of the world would do this.

The Anointed Cherub
(Choreb, Kerub: Plural Cherubim)

The proof of Satan must be that he was the anointed cherub! According to *Webster's Ninth New Collegiate Dictionary*, a cherub is an order of angels.[11] *The American Heritage College Dictionary* defines cherub as "a winged celestial being."[12] In both references, a cherub is described as a small, childlike angel with rosy cheeks and wings. The best reference is found in Gertrude Jobes's *Dictionary of Mythology Folklore and Symbols*, Page 319-320 which describes biblical cherubim as "an order of celestial beings or symbolic representations." Jobes goes on to explain: "The cherubim discern and rule all things and execute with the speed of thought, the will of God, and are messengers representing divine wisdom. They are the powerful transporters of the deity, they are the wind-driven storm clouds which serve as God's chariot, or they themselves are the storm clouds serving as the chariot."(Page 319-320)

The Hebrew ark was surmounted by cherubim, symbolic of the power and protection of God, and the union of the heavenly with the earthly. When shown as two, cherubim are said to symbolize heaven and earth, or the two names of God, Elohim and YAHuVaH (or Yahveh). When shown as four, they represent the four directions or winds—north, south, east, and west.

A cherub is blue or golden, has the form of a winged man with fourfold head—eagle, lion, man, and ox—and stands on wheels. Their eyes represent universal knowledge and omniscience, and their wings represent divine nature and speed. The ox represents the world of cattle, the lion represents wild beasts of the jungle, man represents thinking creatures, and the eagle represents winged creatures. Cherubim are also depicted as winged bulls

---

[11] *Webster's Ninth New Collegiate Dictionary*, s.v. "cherub."
[12] *American Heritage College Dictionary*, 3rd ed., s.v. "cherub."

in Assyria, and as the sphinx, a symbol of protection in Egypt. The best source for understanding cherubim is *Strong's Concordance*.

The king of Tyrus, as an anointed cherub, was a protector whom God had placed in this position, just as He called Moses and Aaron. The Lord was speaking of the king of Tyrus in the first chapter of Amos:

"Thus said the Lord, 'For three transgressions of Tyrus and for four, I will turn away the punishment thereof, because they delivered up the whole captivity of Edom, and remembered not the brotherly covenant'" (Amos 1:9). This verse suggests that Satan had a brother who was mistreated. We are again talking about a king who did not help his neighboring brother's covenant.

God said in verse 10, "But I will send a fire on the walls of [the city] Tyrus, which shall devour the palaces thereof." There is nothing here to suggest a supernatural being of popular belief. The judgment was fire on the city of Tyrus.

God did send a fire and destroyed the city of Tyrus, as we will find out later. The king of Tyrus was a man, not a supernatural fallen angel cast out of heaven. God said of the king, in Ezekiel 28:18, "and I will bring thee to ashes upon the earth," and He did so. Does the king of Tyrus fit the description of a anointed cherub? To anoint someone means to approve of them for a specific purpose or position, to assign them as a protector and keeper. If Satan can be turned to ashes after being in heaven as a supernatural spirit, what is there to say that God would not do it again? Is it possible to enter heaven but later become a rebel and get kicked out and turned into ashes?

Ezekiel 1:4

"And I looked, and, behold, a whirlwind came out of the north, a great cloud, and a fire infolding itself, and brightness was about it, and out of the midst thereof as the color of amber, out of the midst of the fire. Also out of the midst thereof came the likeness of four living creatures. And this was their appearance; they had the likeness of a man. And every one had four faces, and every one had four wings" (Ezekiel 1:4–6).

Notice that each creature stood as man, but each one of the four had four faces. Each head had the face of a man, a lion (on the right side), an ox (on the left side), and an eagle. These living creatures looked like burning coals of fire, as the fire in a lamp. The fire looked as though it was going up and down the creature, and the fire was bright and looked like lightning came from it every so often. (Ezekiel 7:15)

These creatures had four wheels, as wheels in wheels, and it looked like they traveled on their sides. The rings were full of eyes and could travel as fast as light. When the creatures went, the wheels were lifted or folded up over and against them. The spirit of the creatures was in the wheels.

Over their heads, the creatures had something that looked like a sapphire stone (clear glass) or see-through material called the firmament. Ezekiel saw a throne (seat) and a man set upon it. This creature inside the throne looked like fire was running up and down him, like a high voltage charge. (Ezekiel 1:26–27)

This description of a cherub does not fit the king of Tyrus. The cherub was not human, but a device for travel, like a chariot. This is what Ezekiel saw in a vision by the river Chebar in the Spirit—creatures that looked alive and moved quickly in any direction.

Ezekiel 10:6, 19, and 20

This chapter goes a little deeper into what Ezekiel saw. The cherub was on wheels, and the driver seated on the throne or driver's seat told the man clothed with linen, "Go in between the wheels, even under the cherub and fill your hand with coals of fire from between the cherubim and scatter them over the city." The man in linen went and did so, and when the cherubim went, they all four went together. "And the cherubim lifted up their wings and mounted up from the earth in my sight: when they went out, the wheels also were beside them, and every one stood at the door of the east gate of the Lord's house; and the glory of the God of Israel was over them above. This is the living creature that I saw under the God of Israel by the river of Chebar; and I knew that they were the cherubim" (Ezekiel 10:19–20).

It is very clear that the king of Tyrus is not Satan, a supernatural being, as some people believe. The cherub was a way of travel, not an angel. If

Satan is a cherub, then he has wheels, and why would he need wheels to move about if he is supernatural? The fact is that *Satan* is just a word, and a cherub is a device that the God of Israel used to move about.

Psalm 99:1

"The Lord reigneth; let the people tremble: he sitteth between the cherubim; let the earth be moved." The cherubim are the instruments used by God to protect His holiness.

11 Samuel 22:11

"And He [God] rode upon a cherub, and did fly: and he was seen upon the wings of the wind." God had a way of traveling on the wind, clouds on a cherub. The cherubims are the instruments used by God to protect his holiness. "And he [God] rode upon a cherub and did fly: and he was seen upon the wings of the wind." Again this could not be the king of Tyrus as thought to be a supernatural fallen angel by many Christian leaders of today. Can anyone conceive of God riding on the back of an angel, if an angel is a cherub? Thus far, Ezekiel 28 does not prove that the king of Tyrus was Satan or a supernatural being. He was called an anointed cherub because he was a divinely appointed protector.

—— What about Him Being Created? ——

Ezekiel 28:15

"Thou wast perfect in thy ways from the day that thou wast created, till iniquity was found in thee" (Ezekiel 28:15). This description must refer to Adam, since he was the only man to ever be *created*. But does the fact that Adam was created mean that he was Satan, a supernatural being?

To create means "to bring into existence something new," or "create a position in a company or business."[13] For example, the position of king would be created for a responsible person such as Saul or David. But this does not mean that the king was created in the Garden of Eden from the dust of the earth because he had been in Eden. He was perfect when God placed him in that position.

The only record we have of a creation in the Garden of Eden is that of Adam and his wife, Eve. Is he talking about Adam? There can be no fallen angels to be against God and His purpose.

In Revelation 4:11 we read, "Thou art worthy, O Lord to receive glory and honor and power: for thou hast "created" all things, and for thy pleasure they are and were created." God will not allow an angel to come against Him; He would kill that angel at once. Adam knew what he was doing when he took of the fruit in the midst of the garden. In doing so, he disobeyed God and became an adversary or devil toward God in his heart and his action, but he was perfect at his creation until that proving time came.

Isaiah 43:15

"I am the Lord, your holy one, the creator of Israel [Jacob], your king" (Isaiah 43:15). God created Israel by choice. God created Jacob to have priority over his brother in the birthright and blessings.

Isaiah 43:7

"Even everyone that is called by my name: for I have 'Created' him for my glory, I have formed him, yea, I have made him" (Isaiah 43:7). We are created the same way, and God has placed His created ones as pastors, teachers, singers, doctors, firemen, farmers, and more. God has put into your heart what you will do in life. If you disobey, God will deal with you. God creates good and evil for His purposes, as in the case of Pharaoh Thutmose, the third in Moses's day (Romans 9:17).

---

[13] *Webster's Ninth New Collegiate Dictionary*, s.v. "create."

In His Word, God is very clear about who is in charge of this world, regardless of what may be. God is in charge of the affairs of man. "I form the light, and create darkness, I make peace, and create evil, I the Lord do all these things" (Isaiah 45:7). There is no question about who is in charge. It is not a fallen angel or supernatural being.

In Ezekiel 28:8, the king of Tyrus was told that he would be destroyed and dies. He walked in the midst of the stones of fire (the ashes and hot stones of Jerusalem burned) and he took the goods from Jerusalem. God told them that he would set their walls aflame and he would die in the midst of the seas—not in hellfire at the end of time, but down to the pit (verse 10). Those who will do this thing will be a stranger from another ruler. If you believe the king of Tyrus is a supernatural being, a Satan, you should rejoice, because the king of Tyrus is about to be laid to rest. The king took treasures from Jerusalem, and God warned him of his sin and wrongdoing. Now it is payday for him. This Satan is about to meet his creator. The king of Tyrus comes to an end.

Ezekiel 26:1–7

And it came to pass in the eleventh year, in the first day of the month that the word of the Lord came unto me, saying, Son of man, because that Tyrus hath said against Jerusalem, Aha, she is broken that was the gates of the people: she is turned unto me: I shall be replenished, now she is laid waste: Therefore thus saith the Lord God: Behold, I am against thee, O Tyrus, and will cause many nations to come up against thee, as the sea causeth his waves to come up. And they shall destroy the walls of Tyrus [by fire] and break down her towers: I will also scrape her dust from her, and make her like the top of a rock. (Ezekiel 26:1–4)

This included the king of Tyrus and its leaders.

Whom Did God Send to Kill and Destroy Tyrus and the King?

"For thus saith the Lord God: Behold, I will bring upon Tyrus, Nebuchadnezzar King of Babylon, a king of kings, from the north, with horse, and with chariots, and with horsemen, and companies, and much people" (Ezekiel 26:7). All this is about a human king who has the judgment of God coming upon him and will destroy Tyrus. This king of Tyrus was a real king named Ithobalus, or in Hebrew *Ethbaal*. He reigned as king of Tyrus from 878 to 847 BC, and he died in 847 or 846 BC. He was born in 915 BC, served as a priest of Astarte, and had a daughter named Jezebel who was married to King Ahab of northern Israel.[14] James B. Pritchard, *Ancient Near Eastern Text relating to the old testament,* page 475-477, 1969 Wilson, John edition. It is also good to mention that the previous king, King Phelles, was killed by Ithobalus, and his son Baal-Eser, known also as Balbazar and Bal-mazzer, took the throne after the death of his father.

The city of Tyrus was very rich, and its beauty was not the king but the construction works and the towers and temples that were built in Tyrus.

God sent Nebuchadnezzar to destroy Tyrus in 586–573 BC. The reason for this destruction is recorded in Ezekiel 26:12–14. Tyrus's king and its residents had gloated over the fall of Jerusalem, and the king of Tyrus had held back Nebuchadnezzar for thirteen years. But finally Tyrus was captured and destroyed, its walls and high towers were broken down, and Ezekiel was taken into Babylon during the first invasion. Ezekiel was of the middle class but was taken down with the rich. Jeremiah at this time was in Jerusalem praying, and he mourned the destruction of Tyrus. The third invasion occurred in 586 BC. Tyrus today is known as Lebanon, and this is where Solomon got cedar wood to help rebuild the temple in Jerusalem.

The city of Tyre was later captured by Alexandra the Great of Greece. He fulfilled the word of God two hundred years later, to scrape the dust of Tyrus. The island, under Alexander the Great, was annihilated.

---

[14] Pritchard, James B *Ancient Near Eastern Texts. Princeton UP, Page 475-477* 1969, Wilson, A. John Ed.

Jeremiah called Nebuchadnezzar the "destroyer of nations" (Jeremiah 4:7), because he destroyed everything in his path: Phoenicia, Philistia, Judah, Ammon, Moab, and Jerusalem, plus Tyre and others. He captured and looted Jerusalem and was called by the Hebrews "Helel ben Shahar," the shining one, son of the dawn.

The king of Tyrus was put down by the army of Nebuchadnezzar. As God said, he was a man and he was to die in seas. There is nothing to suggest that the king of Tyrus was Satan; he was only a man.

During these years of wars, the years between 887 and 856 BC, Israel's king Ahab married Jezebel, the daughter of the Tyrus King Ethbaal, who introduced the cult of the Phoenician gods Baal and Ashtoreth or Astarte to Israel. Jezebel was killed in 841 BC by King Jehu of Israel (2 Kings 9:10).

The king of Tyrus submitted to Nebuchadnezzar, and the royal family departed to Babylon. About thirteen years later, a delegation of judges who ruled Tyrus came to Babylon and asked Nebuchadnezzar if he would send their king, Merbaal, back to Tyrus. Nebuchadnezzar agreed to do so. Merbaal died four years later, and then his son Hiram reigned for twenty years. God had sent Nebuchadnezzar to take down Tyrus and destroy all its glory because Tyrus had boasted of the fall of Jerusalem, and Nebuchadnezzar did his work quite well. Hiram, King of Tyrus, and Solomon were close. The story of King Hiram of Tyrus is recorded in 1 Kings, beginning in chapter 5, and in 2 Chronicles 2:1–18. (Hiram is also spelled Huram.)

There can be no doubt that the king of Tyrus was all human, because he died. He was mortal—not a supernatural angel cast out of heaven, as some people teaches.

Lucifer's Origin: How Did Lucifer Become Satan?

The average church tries very hard to prove the existence of a supernatural being, not knowing that Lucifer is not a person and never was. The only place he appears is Isaiah 14:12: "How art thou fallen from heaven, O Lucifer, son of the morning, How art thou cut down to the ground, which didst weaken the nations?"

Where Did the Word Lucifer Come From and What Is Its Meaning?

We talked about Lucifer earlier in this work in the section titled "Are Devils Fallen Angels?" *Lucifer* is a Latin word. We don't know how the word got into a Hebrew manuscript. However, Lucifer was a king—not Satan or a fallen angel. The story of Lucifer is all about a king who persecuted the children of Israel.

Roman astronomy shows that *Lucifer* was the name of the morning star that we call Venus. It is a star that can be seen in the morning before dawn or the rising of the sun.

You can see how easy it would be to have a mix-up. We had the Catholic students of the Bishop Bible and other groups using the Vulgate Bible by Jerome in making the King James Bible. They cut and pasted until they had a Bible that everyone could agree on. At best, it was a fast job. The King James Bible is basically a Catholic Bible rewritten, because there was another Bible being published and the rush was on to hit the king's desk first. The new King James Bible was mostly the writing of the Bishop and the Vulgate versions, with no references to the Hebrew text.

Jerome's Vulgate mistranslated the Hebrew text *Day Star*, son of the dawn, as Lucifer. Years later Lucifer became a person, a disobedient angel cast out of heaven. The ancient Latin describes the morning star, the bringer of light. The Hebrew passage reads, "heleyl Ben Shachar" which was translated as "the shining one, son of dawn"—literally, the planet Venus.

Let us read it from the Hebrew Bible: "How did you come to fall from the heaven, morning star, son of the dawn?" (Isaiah 14:12).[15] *The Life Application Bible* reads, "How you are fallen from heaven, O day star, son of dawn: How you are cut down to the ground, you who laid nations low."

The King James Bible only carries the name Lucifer, which was a mistranslation from the Vulgate Bible. It is very hard for the church to accept *Lucifer* as just a word that means nothing more than a day star or morning star, Venus. It is especially hard for readers of the King James Bible to accept this. Lucifer has to be a devil, according to the teaching of

---

[15] Stern, David H. *Complete Jewish Bible.*

today, but it would be nice if they would look up the Latin word and see for themselves.

Why Does the Church Believe Isaiah ——— 14:12 to Be Lucifer, the Devil, a ——— Supernatural Being Cast Out of Heaven?

The church[16] believes this based on the following:

1. The Christian church believes Lucifer is Satan. Many people will not research the word *Lucifer*, nor do they seek to understand the subject of this chapter. (Isaiah 14:12)
2. "For thou hast said in thine heart, I will ascend into heaven, I will exalt my throne above the stars of God: I will sit also upon the mount of the congregation, in the sides of the north" (Isaiah 14:13). Stars are priests or ministers of God. (Also see Revelation 12:4, 1:20, and 3:1.)
3. "I will ascend above the heights of the clouds; I will be like the most High." (Isaiah 14:14).

In this chapter we are talking about Babylon's king Nebuchadnezzar, who had great power. He was known as a king of kings and had captured several cities. God used Nebuchadnezzar as a rod and sword against the king of Tyrus, destroying the city in a thirteen-year war lasting from 586 to 573 BC. Isaiah 14:4 says, "That thou shalt take up this proverb against the King of Babylon, and say, how hath the oppressor ceased! The golden city ceased!"

Isaiah called the king "son of the morning," not "Lucifer." Lucifer means "son of the dawn, the morning star, or bringer of light." The word *Lucifer* is Latin, not Hebrew or Greek. The word was used by Jerome to refer only to the morning star, Venice. Lucifer was a mythological Canaanite god called Attar; in the Vulgate, the word is Hailail (Hailil).

---

[16] *Church* is being used as a generic term to represent today's average church of the fundamental faith.

Theodorent of Cyrus wrote that Isaiah called King Nebuchadnezzar the "Morning Star" only because he had the illusion of being just that, in 393–457 BC records. The French, Germans, Portuguese, Spanish, the Vulgate, and Martin Luther all agreed that *Lucifer* refers only to Venice, the morning star or day star, not to a devil or Satan of supernatural power. Lucifer is not found in any Hebrew scriptures.

Isaiah 14:13 says, "For thou hast said in thine heart." It was in the king of Babylon's heart to do these things, but that doesn't prove that he actually could. Only a supernatural being such as Satan or an angel could do these things, at any time and as often as they desired. The heart of King Nebuchadnezzar was evil, and the Lord was reminding him that what was in his heart wasn't acceptable and would bring about God's judgment. What a person thinks in their heart, God hears aloud—and He will respond.

Nebuchadnezzar said that he would ascend into heaven, exalt his throne above the stars of God, ascend above the clouds, and be like the Most High. He appeared to be unstoppable. He had machines of war and a great army that was feared by many people. He had won a victory over Jerusalem, stolen all the vessels of the Lord's house, and captured the people as slaves. And yet he respected the Hebrew's God as related to judgment. When Nebuchadnezzar captured the city of Jerusalem, he found Jeremiah sitting in jail—and he let him go.

Nebuchadnezzar boasted about how powerful he was and how he had destroyed their God's house and beheaded many of the people. And he said that when he died, he would take over God's kingdom and kill Him.

Daniel 2:37

"Thou, O King, art a king of kings: for the God of heaven hath given thee a kingdom, power, and strength, and glory" (Daniel 2:37). This kingdom was given to King Nebuchadnezzar by God and he was very much human—called the son of dawn, not a Lucifer or Satan of supernatural origin. Did he fulfill his heart's desire? Yes, he did.

1. He was lifted up above all men, although not to where God is.
2. He was seated as a god.

3. He was worshipped as a god.
4. And he sat at the most high, if only in his heart.

Daniel 3:5

"That at what time ye hear the sound of the cornet, flute, harp, sackbut, psaltery, dulcimer, and all kinds of music, ye fall down and worship the golden image that Nebuchadnezzar the king hath set up" (Daniel 3:5). Why would a king think in his heart to do those things listed in Isaiah 14:13? Pride! He believes he created himself of his own power and means.

Daniel 4:17 says "This matter is by the decree of the watchers, and the demand by the word of the holy ones: to the intent that the living may know that the most High ruleth in the kingdom of men, and giveth it to whomsoever he will, and sitteth up over it the basest of men."

Anyone who sets himself up as something special above the people around him, whether he's a king or a man on the street, should know that the Lord is always looking and judging the hearts of man. The Most High is in control, despite rulers in the kingdom of men. Daniel told King Nebuchadnezzar that he would be forced to live like an ox until he learned that "the most High ruleth in the kingdom of men, and giveth it to whomsoever he will" (Daniel 4:25). We don't rule, create ourselves, or build kingdoms on our own. Daniel also said, in verse 26, "the heavens do rule." How clear this is.

"The king spake, and said, is not this great Babylon, that I have built for the house of the kingdom, by the might of my power, and for the honor of my majesty?" (Daniel 4:30). If this king was Lucifer or Satan, a supernatural being, why do we see him living like an animal? That is, until he learned that God is in control of—and rules in—the kingdom of men.

For seven years, God keep Nebuchadnezzar out of power. He ate grass in the fields like an ox, until he *knew* that God was ruler in the land and that he had fallen because of his pride. After Nebuchadnezzar's death, the kingdom fell under the kingship of Belshazzar, when God sent the Medes and Persians to capture the great city of Babylon.

But Belshazzar had set himself up against God. Daniel 5:23 says, "But hath lifted up thyself against the Lord of heaven: and they have brought the vessels of his house before thee, and thou, and thy Lords, thy wives, and thy concubines, have drunk wine in them: and thou hast praised the gods of silver, and gold, of brass, iron, wood, and stone, which see not, nor hear, nor know: and the God in whose hand thy breath is, and whose are all thy ways, hast thou not glorified." That night Belshazzar was killed by the Medians. His wife also died, probably from grief.

The student of the Bible can plainly see that these kings of Isaiah 14:12 are all human, not supernatural. Nor are they Satan, because of the word *Lucifer*, which comes from the words *lux* (light, fire) and *ferre* (to bear, to bring). The Statue of Liberty is a bringer of light, and thus is a "Lucifer."

Revelation 12:5

(1) "And she brought forth a man child, who was to rule all nations with a Rod of Iron: and her child was caught up unto God, and to his throne" (Revelation 12:5). The child is caught up to heaven, where we find the dragon engaged in a war with Michael and the angels. The dragon is expelled, falls to earth, and chases the woman but is unable to catch her. The dragon then discharges a flood of water from his mouth, intending to drown her, but the earth opens, the water sinks, and the woman is saved. If John was seeing into the future, who was this child, if not Christ? Was this writing before the ascension of Jesus, and was it carried to Patmos with John and kept with him until he was freed from Patmos?

—— Was the Devil Ever in Heaven? ——

(2) Son of man, take up a lamentation upon the King of Tyrus, and say unto him, "Thus said the Lord God, Thou sealest up the sum, full of wisdom, and perfect in beauty. Thou hast been in Eden the garden of God, every precious stone was thy covering, the sardius, topaz, and the diamond, the beryl, the onyx, and the jasper, the sapphire, the emerald, and the carbuncle, and the gold: the workmanship of thy tablets and of thy pipes was

prepared in thee in the day that thou wast created. Thou art the anointed cherub that covereth, and I have set thee so: thou wast upon the holy mountain of God; thou hast walked up and down in the midst of the stones of fire. Thou wast perfect in thy ways from the day that thou wast created, till iniquity was found in thee." (Ezekiel 28:15–15)

(3) Christians who believe in a personal devil also use Isaiah 14:12–15: "How art thou fallen from heaven, O Lucifer, son of the morning! How art thou cut down to the ground, which didst weaken the nations! For thy hast said in thine heart, I will ascend into heaven, I will exalt my throne above the stars of God: I will sit also upon the mount of the congregation, in the sides of the North. I will ascend above the heights of the clouds; I will be like the most High."

The scriptures we have just read provide even less proof of a supernatural devil than the previously read passages from Revelation 12. In both cases, however, a human being is being addressed—either the king of Babylon (Nebuchadnezzar) or the prince of Tyre (Ithobaal). Educated ministers have a problem with these scriptures. They apply the word *devil* to Nebuchadnezzar, the king of Tyrus, Lucifer, and the prince of Tyrus. If there is a personal devil called Satan, how can he be all these kings at the same time in history?

We have already discussed the origins of the words *devil* and *Satan*. *Devil* was originally Greek and is found only in the New Testament. *Satan* is Hebrew, and then Greek by adoption. English dictionaries give us the meanings of these words as currently understood, as a fallen angel, the enemy of God and man. But how can we, as Christians, understand the Word of God in its original tongue and language, rather than as it is interpreted in modern English?

Satan as an Angel

In the Hebrew Bible, the first place where *adversary* or *Satan* occurs is in Numbers: "And God's anger was kindled because he [Balaam] went, and the angel of the Lord stood in the way for an adversary [Satan] against him" (Numbers 22:22). We associate the word *devil* with a particular type of character, as in, "That devil just got out of jail." It had nothing to do with being a supernatural being.

"And the angel of the Lord said unto him, 'Wherefore hast thou smitten thine ass these three times? Behold, I went out to withstand thee'" (Numbers 22:32). The angel was acting as an adversary, a Satan. Satan was a holy angel! Then is it possible that God, in some cases, acts as a devil against an individual? *Satan* in English is untranslated, and is treated as a person using the masculine forms of Hebrew and Greek.

As we read in 2 Samuel 19:22, "And David said, what have I to do with you, ye sons of Zeruiah, that ye should this day be adversaries [Satan] unto me?" David knew that these people were trouble from the start and that their hearts were not dedicated to the work of the Lord.

"But now the Lord my God hath given me rest on every side so that there is neither adversary [Satan] nor evil occurrent" (1 Kings 5:4). The term *adversary* is used quite often, as in 1 Kings 11:14: "And the Lord stirred up an adversary [Satan] unto Solomon, Hadad the Edomite: he was of the King's seed in Edom." The Lord was responsible for Solomon's adversaries, but his adversary was Hadad, the king's seed, not a supernatural being cast out of heaven. Hadad was an adversary (Satan) to Solomon. (Incidentally, it was the Edomite priest who gave Christ so much trouble.)

Adversary appears again in chapter 11 of 1 Kings: "And God stirred him up another adversary [Satan], Rezon the son of Eliadah, which fled from his Lord Hadadezer king of Zobah" (1 Kings 11:23). In this case, Rezon became a Satan, along with Hadad—two adversaries, two *Satans*, who stirred people up to make trouble. "And he was an adversary to Israel all the days of Solomon" (1 Kings: 11:25). This is what God did to Solomon, a very wise man of God.

Translators have been very careful in their use of the words *Satan* and *adversary*, and how they have been placed in scripture. In translating scripture from Hebrew into English, they replaced the original word *adversary* with *Satan*. In doing so, they maintained the masculine gender of the Greek and kept the word *Satan* to refer to a personal devil. This became the popular theory of Satan, which exists to this very day among Christian churches.

Who Was the Satan That Caused Job Such Terror?

When we think of Job, we also think of the trials that he suffered. Job lost everything because of his dealings with what some people call Satan or the devil. However, it is more accurate to say that Job's *adversaries* brought him down and caused him to curse the day he was born.

Job's enemies were called sons of God, but does that mean they were from heaven? No, they were sons of God as we see the phrase used in 1 John 3:2: "Beloved, now are we the sons of God." This demonstrates that to be sons of God, you do not have to be a supernatural fallen angel; you can be just a flesh-and-blood human being.

The Satan (adversary) of Job had his eyes on Job's estate and also affected Job's body. This Satan, no doubt, was one of the sons of God who envied Job's lifestyle and desired to bring him to ruin.

Job

The book of Job is used by the church in its attempt to prove that Satan is a fallen angel, cast out of heaven after fighting against Michael. This was to have happened before or during the time of Noah. However, in chapter 12 of Revelation, the wonders and war described were to take place shortly, and after John. In Revelation 4:1, we find the phrase, "which must be hereafter." If John was written about 95 AD, it had to be after that. So when did Satan supposedly be cast out of heaven?

Before we go further, we should study Job's ordeal with God and his enemies. The book of Job was written by Moses. Job was born six hundred years after the flood of Noah's day, and he was ninety-one years old when Joseph was sold into Egypt. Job died at the age of 210, or fifteen years before Moses led the Jews out of Egypt.

— Is Job's Satan a Supernatural Being? —

Many Christians believe that the story of Job supports this idea, but the King James Bible does not agree in the word of the scripture with the Hebrew text.

The dates of Job are not clear, but we do have some information that may be helpful on this subject. Job was the grandson of Esau and his second wife was Dinah, Jacob's daughter. Job was also believed to be known by some as Jobab, king of Edom, but this isn't definite.

Eliphaz was the son of Esau, and Bildad, Zophar, and Elihu were sons of Shuah, Naamat, and Barachel, who was the son of Buz, brother of Job and nephew of Abraham. Esau was fifteen years old at Abraham's death. Job was born after Abraham and during the time of the twelve sons of Jacob known as Israel, who were chosen by the Lord to be his firstborn sons, thus making them sons of God.

Jacob is believed to have lived around 1800 BC, Isaac around 2006 BC, and Job around 2000–1700 BC, although these dates might not be accurate. We do know that the law of Moses was not known at this time. Job was knowledgeable of the flood of Noah's day, which is mentioned in Job 22:15–16: "Hast thou marked the old way which wicked men have trodden [walked]? Which were cut down out of time, whose foundation was over flown with a flood?" In the Jewish Bible, we read, "Are you going to keep to the old way, the one the wicked have trodden, and the ones snatched away before their time, whose foundations a flood swept way?"[17] (The complete Jewish Bible, (Job 22:15-16 page 1019). There is no mention here of fallen angels, only of wicked people.

Job 1:6

"Now there was a day when the sons of God came to present themselves before the Lord, and Satan came also among them" (Job 1:6). The King James should translate *Satan* as *adversary*, as used in the Hebrew Bible, rather than turning Satan into a person and using *adversary* to refer to any

---

[17] Stern, David H. *Complete Jewish Bible.pp1019*

person. *Strong's Concordance* does not say Satan is a person, but instead uses the word to describe any person or event that would hinder someone from pursuing their goals for Christ. Moses was a Satan to Pharaoh, and he had powers similar to Job's Satan, as recorded in Exodus 4:21. God gave them the power to afflict.

Job 2:1 tells us that "Again there was a day when the sons of God came to present themselves before the Lord, and Satan came also among them to present himself before the Lord." But the Hebrew text says an unnamed "adversary" came, not Satan.

We do not know when the sons of God presented themselves. The Bible says that this was the second time they met, after the flood had re-created the earth. The King James Bible uses the masculine word *Satan*, not *adversary*, which suggests that this Satan was, in fact, a person. However, it does not prove that this person was a son of God in supernatural form. Let us read the text in two different ways.

(1) Job 2:1 tells us that "Again there was a day when the sons of God came to present themselves before the Lord, and Satan came also among them to present himself before the Lord." This gives the reader the sense of Satan being a specific, individual person.

(2) Here's the same passage in Stern's *Complete Jewish Bible*: "Another day came when the sons of God came to serve Adonai, and among them came the adversary to serve Adonai." The word *adversary* is used, rather than *Satan*. The adversary was not being adversarial toward God, but rather toward Job. Among all the people in that region, all the cattleman or herdsmen, only Job was a concern to the individual Satan or adversary.

We can present ourselves to God only through prayer, since no one can look directly at God and live. The meeting described in Job 2:1 was not a face-to-face conversation with God, nor was the meeting in heaven before God. As one of the sons of God, Satan can do no harm on his own; his power can come only from God. Job's problem was all about his wealth. The sons of God never saw God face-to-face—and Satan is a word, not a person.

Exodus 34:2

"And be ready in the morning, and come up in the morning unto Mount Sinai, and present thyself there to Me in the top of the mount" (Exodus 34:2). When Moses presented himself and talked with God, he did as just as he had talked to the angel of the Lord at the burning bush, just as in the case of the sons of God and Satan. He presented himself as the priest did in the Holy of Holies at the Ark of the Covenant, where the priest and God communicated.

Leviticus 14:11

"And the priest that maketh him clean shall present the man that is to be made clean, and those things, before the Lord, at the door of the tabernacle of the congregation" (Leviticus 14:11). Being in the presence of the Lord means to be where He tells you to meet Him. God is always present and His eyes are everywhere, but He is an unseen Spirit (see John 4:24).

The term *sons of God* do not always refer to the angels of God in heaven. Throughout history, ancient Eastern kings, such as Egypt's pharaohs, are known to have been referred to as "sons" of particular gods. For example, Akhenaton reduced the pharaoh's role to that of coregent, where the pharaoh and God ruled as father and son, and he took on the role of priest of God.

The Jewish kings were often called sons of the Lord. However, references to sons of God don't appear in the Tanakh; instead, the Lord speaks to the king, telling him that he is His son. The whole house of Israel was God's firstborn son (see Jeremiah 31:9). In Job, the sons of God were people recognized as leaders—priests or kings, not angels from heaven. Sons of God can be both heavenly and earthly.

In 42 BC, Julius Caesar was deified as *Divus Julius* (the divine Julius) after his death. Fifteen years later, in 27 BC, his son Octavian, better known as Augustus, received the title of *Divi Juli filius* (son of the Divine Julius) or son of the gods.

In Exodus 4:22, God gave Jacob (Israel) the title of his firstborn: "And thou shalt say unto Pharaoh, Thus saith the Lord, Israel is my son, even my firstborn." This is an example of a human son of God.

In Psalm 89:26–27, David recorded these words: "He shall cry unto me, 'Thou art my Father, my God, and the rock of my salvation.' I also will make him my firstborn, higher than the kings of the earth." David called God his father, and God calls David His firstborn. In 2 Samuel 7:14, God says of David, "I will be his father and he shall be my son." We now have Israel, David, and Ephraim as God's firstborn—sons of God. All are flesh and blood men serving on earth, not spirits or angels in heaven. In the New Testament, we also find Jesus Christ called the son of God, the difference being that He is the first begotten son of God. In fact, when anyone accepts Christ as Lord and Savior, as John tells us in 1 John 3:2, "Beloved, Now are we the sons of God."

These scriptures should be proof enough that the "sons of God" in Job do not have to be angels from heaven, but are instead people who serve the living God here on earth. These sons of God could be the leaders of the house of Israel, the twelve sons of Jacob, which would fit the time of Job and his family. In fact, this may be how Moses knew about the story of Job. Moses heard from Korah about his matter and Korah told Moses "all the congregation are holy, every one of them." (Numbers 16:3) In Exodus 19:6, God says that Israel is "a kingdom of priest, and an holy nation." Now, if they are holy, as the Bible says in Ezekiel 18:4, "Behold, all souls are mine: as the soul of the father, so also the soul of the son is mine: the soul that sinneth, it shall die."

We can conclude from these scriptures that we all belong to God as children. Whether holy or unholy, we are all sons of God and we all have a choice about how to live and die.

Abraham and Isaac was not the house of Israel; they were family members of Jacob. But it was Jacob whose name was changed to Israel after he wrestled with the angel of the Lord. The "house of Israel" always refers to the twelve sons of Jacob. Abraham, Lot, and Job were from the land of Uz, which God told Abraham to leave. This being an area of Edom, the land was named after one of the sons of Dishan. Since Job lived in Uz, he was probably an Edomite. He was a rich ruler in the community, possibly even a king.

Eliphaz, Bildad, and Zophar were close to Job. These three mighty men in the community found Job in a bad situation, watched him, and finally told him that his problems were caused by his sin. Job's business fell apart, and his family, hired hands, and livestock were all killed. At one point, Job wished he would die.

The sons of God would be those who serve and worship the Lord—the sons of Jacob, leaders of the house of Israel, and one of Job's friends, Eliphaz, who was the son of Esau.

Job's adversary asked God to leave Job alone. Job was serving God, because of the wealth with which he had been blessed. His adversary asked God to step back and remove His hedge of protection from around Job, because Job would then stop serving God. The adversary asked God to remove Himself and His protection from Job.

The Lord told the adversary that Job was all right, a good man. "But put forth thine hand now, and touch all that he hath, and he will curse thee to thy face" (Job 1:11). Job may have never had any hard times in his life, and people wanted to see if Job could handle it, not being rich and losing everything.

The Lord's Response

"And the Lord said unto Satan, 'Behold, all that he hath is in thy power; only upon himself put not forth thine hand" (Job 1:12). Satan did this on several occasions, but Job held fast to his integrity. After Satan left Job, nothing else is heard from Satan; it was a waiting game.

Job's real enemy was his own heart, and his own thoughts brought about his trouble. "For the thing which I greatly feared is come upon me and that which I was afraid of is come unto me" (Job 3:25). Job talks about all the things the Lord is doing to him. There was not a supernatural Satan, only a fear in his heart that he may lose it all. And in the end, Job says, "Though He slay me, yet will I trust him" (Job 13:15). It was all about Job and the Lord.

After the adversary showed up and tested Job all those times, who was it that the Lord rebuked? Not a supernatural devil, but three men: Eliphaz, Bildad and Zophar. They were Job's real adversaries, the three men who had accused Job of sinning.

Reading from the Complete Jewish Bible, the Tanakh,[18] we see that Eliphaz accused Job: "For you kept your kinsman's goods as collateral for no reason, you stripped the poorly clothed of what they have, you didn't give water to the weary to drink, you withheld food from the hungry" (Job 22:6–7). Job was accused of living the way that people had lived before the flood: "Are you going to keep to the old way, the one the wicked have trodden?" (Job 22:15). Those people were snatched away before their time, swept away by the flood. They had said to God, Leave us alone.

In Job 18:19, Bildad said of Job, "Without son or nephew among his people, no one will remain in his dwelling." Job had lost everything, and as Bildad said in Job 18:21, "This is how things are in the house of the wicked [sinners], and this is the place of those who don't know God." And Zophar said to Job, "If you will set your heart right, if you will spread out your hands toward him, if you will put your iniquity at a distance and not let unrighteousness remain in your tents, then when you lift up your face, there will be no defect, you will be firm and free from fear" (Job 11:13–15, Tanakh). Job was told that his problems were of his own making. But this story goes on to say that the Lord rebuked the three friends of Job and told them that if they would get their act together, Job would pray for them and they would be forgiven.

The story of Job is all about everyday people in everyday life situations. In this particular case, the sons of God were people and this Satan was a person. Job brought his problems on himself, and God allowed that to happen. There isn't anything in Job to suggest that Satan, a supernatural being from heaven, caused Job's problems! The Lord allowed this to happen to Job, but He rebuked Eliphaz because he and his two friends spoke to Job and lied against the Lord, which was not true and right. Because of their lies, the Lord rebuked the Satan who was Eliphaz, Bildad, and Zophar (see Job 42:7–8).

[18] Kerns, David H., ed., *The Complete Jewish Bible*. 1998, Messianic Jewish publishers MD Job 22:6-7,11:13-15

What About the Calamities of Tempest and Disease That Befell Job?

These events that fell upon Job were controlled by the power of God, not by the adversary so well known by the church as Satan. God said, "Thou movest me against him to destroy him without cause" (Job 2:3). God inflicted the calamities on Job at the adversary's request.

Job makes a plea to those around him: "Have pity upon me, o ye, my friends, for the hand of God hath touched me" (Job 19:21). Job, at the end of his trouble. "Then came there unto him all his brethren, and all his sisters, and all they that had been of his acquaintance before, and did eat bread with him in his house and they bemoaned him and comforted him over all the evil that the Lord had brought upon him" (Job 42:11). The family and friends came together, as well as the adversaries. Nothing else is heard of Satan, and all the evil ended. Job had no more problems after his family and friends came together and started to love each other again. This is a great lesson to learn, that all your blessings are from the Lord and He is in charge, whether you keep it or not. As Job said, the Lord giveth and the Lord taketh away.

If the adversary (Satan) had the power to attack Job, it does not prove him to be a supernatural agent. God permitted Moses the power to turn his rod to a serpent, and Moses was just an average human being working for God. Who opened the Red Sea? God did, through His servant Moses. God can and does delegate miraculous power even to mortal man.

- Scripture in Which Satan Is Untranslated -

We read in 1 Chronicles 21:1, "And Satan stood up against Israel, and provoked David to number Israel." Again in Psalm 109:6, "Set thou a wicked man over him: and let Satan stand at his right hand." In the Hebrew text there is no indication of a personal devil, only an adversary with an evil intent. "And he showed me Joshua the High Priest standing before the angel of the Lord, and Satan standing at his right hand to resist him. And the Lord said unto Satan. The Lord rebuke thee, O Satan, even the Lord that hath chosen Jerusalem" (Zechariah 3:1–2).

In Psalm 109:6, the first untranslated text, we make reference to 2 Samuel 24:1 and 1 Chronicles 21:1, in which Satan was God Himself. In 1 Chronicles 21:1, "Satan stood up against Israel, and provoked David to number Israel." Was this Satan a supernatural being? Does the Bible clear this matter up? Yes, we find in 2 Samuel 24:1, "And again the anger of the Lord was kindled against Israel, and He [God] moved David against them to say, go, number Israel and Judah." Not a fallen angel.

The angel of God was a Satan to Balaam, as we have seen, and in that case, God proved a Satan to Israel and would be considered a supernatural being. Moved by a perverse people, God's Spirit moved on David and caused the calamity to the nation by numbering the people.

Ezra 4:1

Ezra 3:2 says, "Then stood up Joshua the son of Jozadak, and his brethren the priests, and Zerubbabel the son of Shealtiel, and his brethren, and builded the altar of the God of Israel, to offer burnt offerings thereon, as it is written in the law of Moses the man of God." In Ezra 3:2–3, the work was taking place to build the altar and to perform the burnt offering as commanded, and they did so and were rejoicing. During this rejoicing, the laborers were laying the new foundation of the temple, and they completed it in a ceremony of shouts.

> Now when the adversaries [Satan's] of Judah and Benjamin heard that the children of the captivity builded the temple unto the Lord God of Israel, then they came to Zerubbabel, and to the chief of the fathers, and said unto them, "Let us build with you ..." But Zerubbabel and Joshua and the rest of the chief of the fathers of Israel, said unto them, "Ye have nothing to do with us to build an house unto our God; but we ourselves together will build unto the Lord God of Israel, as King Cyrus the King of Persia hath commanded us." Then the people of the land weakened the hands of the people of Judah, and troubled them in building, and hired counselors against them,

to frustrate their purpose, all the days of Cyrus King of Persia, even until the reign of Darius King of Persia. (Ezra 4:1–5)

The churches who insist upon the popular Satan having to do with the matter have to prove the existence of such a being first, before the passage from Zachariah can help them. Disobedience will bring death (Leviticus 10:1–2). It is important to remember that *Satan* is a word—the definition of the word *adversary*—and not a personality.

Satan Means Only Adversary

The Hebrew word *Satan* was adopted into the Greek language and every Greek word is either masculine, feminine, or neutral. We understand that few will take the time to research this subject, but without haste will try to defend their position not knowing the subject.

The Greeks used the word *Satan* in their text of the New Testament, but we know that Satan is only a Hebrew word that means "adversary." The word *devil* is also used in the New Testament, sometimes interchangeably with *Satan*.

What about the statement Jesus made to the church at Pergamos? Pergamos was one of the seven churches of Asia that John wrote about while on Patmos.

Revelation 2:13 says, "I know thy works, and where thou dwellest, even where Satan's seat is: and thou holdest fast my name, and hast not denied my faith, even in those days wherein Antipas was my faithful martyr, who was slain among you, where Satan dwelleth."

This Satan, living in the day of John, was a human king or priest. This was while John was on the island of Patmos in the days of John the apostle's exile. Satan's headquarters were Pergamos, in Asia Minor. Pergamos was populated mostly by people who were enemies of the truth and quick to persecute the believers of Christ. We see Satan's seat and the dwelling place of Satan (the adversary) to be earthly and not heavenly.

We're spending a lot of time on the subject of Satan the adversary, because some people have a hard time understanding the scriptures and what they mean. It is only fair that we make every possible effort to demonstrate biblical truth, and maybe we'll lead someone to understand that their life is between God and the people around them, and not a personal devil.

Was Peter a Satan?

In Matthew 16:23 we read, "But he turned, and said unto Peter, Get thee behind me Satan: thou art an offence unto me, for thou savourest not the things that be of God, but those that be of man." Peter's protest against the sacrifice of Christ was considered to be the action of an enemy. Jesus's death was necessary to give us salvation, so opposing His death made Peter a Satan in a biblical sense. In Matthew 8:33, Jesus said, "For thou savourest not the things that be of God, but the things that be of men." Jesus was telling Peter that he was acting like a carnal man who didn't have the heart to do God's will.

To be an adversary against God is to be Satan, since "adversary" is the definition of the word *Satan*.[19] Peter was a man and a Satan who later became Christ's leading apostle, after conversion by the renewing of his mind. After his conversion, Paul suffered many things because of following Jesus, more so than any other disciple. Paul tried to warn the follows of Christ about people in the city who wanted to cause trouble for Christ.

In 1 Timothy 1:2, Paul said, "Of whom is Hymenaeus and Alexander, whom I have delivered unto Satan that they may learn not to blaspheme." What a profound statement to be made by Paul. The scripture provides plenty of evidence to disprove the orthodox Satan, which many Christians have accepted as a supernatural being who opposes God in the New Testament. Paul said he turned Hymenaeus and Alexander over to Satan to learn not to blaspheme. How did he do that? Paul employs Satan to teach these guys a lesson, not to blaspheme. Who ever heard of a Christian turning other Christians over to Satan to be taught how not to blaspheme?

"For I verily, as absent in body, but present in spirit have judged already, as though I were present concerning him who hath so done this

---

[19] *Strong's Concordance* H7853.

deed, in the name of our Lord Jesus Christ, when ye are gathered together, and my spirit, with the power of our Lord Jesus Christ, to deliver such a one unto Satan, for the destruction of the flesh that the spirit may be saved in the day of the Lord Jesus" (1 Corinthians 5:3–5). Paul is responding to the church because of a letter he received about a young man who had sex with his stepmother, and Paul responded with a letter of excommunication.

Paul's letter to the church showed that this was not a single event. In 1 Corinthians 5:1 we read, "It is reported commonly that there is fornication among you and such fornication as is not so much named among the Gentiles, that one should have his father's wife." Paul was saying simply that the offender must be removed from the community of believers and dismissed from the church as an undesirable example. Paul says in 1 Corinthians 5:2, "Ye are puffed up, and having not rather mourned, that he that hath done this deed might be taken away from among you," and he concludes in verse 13, "Put away from among yourselves that wicked person." This would be the same as a Satan among the church members.

"And if any man obey not our word by this epistle, note that man, and have no company with him, that he may be ashamed. Yet count him not as an enemy, but admonish him as a brother" (2 Thessalonians 3:14–15). Paul is telling them to turn the man over to Satan, instead of hanging around with him and being judged by his lifestyle. "Love not the world" (1 John 2:15). Lust was of the flesh and therefore was condemned.

In 1 Corinthians 5:5, Paul tells us that he has decided "to deliver such a one unto Satan for the destruction of the flesh that the spirit may be saved in the day of the Lord Jesus." This is not to kill the individual, but to destroy the carnal thinking that was in their midst. Paul tells the Corinthians, "Purge out therefore the old leaven that ye may be a new lump, as ye are unleavened" (1 Corinthians 5:7).

When Paul says, "Put away from among yourselves that wicked person" (1 Corinthians 5:13), he uses the same terminology that was applied to Peter by Jesus. This was one way the early Christians preserved their faith and held themselves to a higher standard. Similarly, when Paul says, "Wherefore we would have come unto you, even I Paul, once and again, but Satan hindered us," he isn't speaking of a supernatural spirit, but of people filled with hatred and evil hearts (1 Thessalonians 2:18).

Who Hindered Paul? Was It Satan, Who Was Cast Out of Heaven?

Those who hindered Paul were people who hated the truth. Paul identified such people as *Satan*, adversaries who hindered him and would have liked to kill him. On one occasion, when Paul was in prison, he actually named a Satan that hindered him. Paul was writing about how some had left him and why he had sent others away. "Alexander the Coppersmith did me much evil: the Lord rewards him according to his works. Of whom be thou ware also, for he hath greatly withstood our words" (2 Timothy 4:14–15).

Paul said Alexander the coppersmith did not agree with him and did not desire to hear what he had to say. This Satan or devil was not a supernatural being, but a person who did everything possible to shut Paul down.

2 Timothy 3:8

"Now as Jannes and Jambres withstood Moses, so do these also resist the truth: men of corrupt minds, reprobate concerning the faith" (2 Timothy 3:8). Paul said that such people (Satan, devils) resist the truth because they "have a form of godliness but [deny] the power thereof, from such turn way" (2 Timothy 3:5). "And their word will eat as doth a canker: of whom is Hymenaeus and Philetus" (2 Timothy 2:17). Once again, these Satan's and devils are people who oppose the truth, and Paul doesn't hesitate to name them.

Paul said these people are preaching in error, teaching that the resurrection has already passed. This could be the experience some people had at the resurrection of the dead, when Christ was nailed to the cross. Some people in the graves came alive and walked through town, and they were recognized. This could well be the problem Paul had with Hymenaeus and Philetus; unlike Paul, they might have witnessed the resurrection of the dead. But the Satan and devils of the orthodox teaching of today have nothing to do with Paul's problem.

— Does This Prove a Supernatural Being? —

"And after the sop Satan entered into him. Then Jesus said unto him, that thou doest, do quickly" (John 13:27). Satan entering Judas is not a supernatural demon, as some suppose. Jesus knew what was in the heart of Judas and He also knew that Judas had to be the one to betray Him. It was necessary for the plan of salvation of the world. If Judas had not betrayed Jesus, how would salvation have come about?

Jesus gave Judas a morsel of bread and said, "One of you shall betray me" (John 13:21). This shocked the group and created an emotional stir. Then we read that John, "lying on Jesus breast said unto him, Lord, who is it? Jesus answered, He it is to whom I shall give a sop, when I have dipped it. And when he had dipped the sop, he gave it to Judas Iscariot, the son of Simon. And after the sop Satan entered into" (John 13:25–27). Does this prove that Judas was a supernatural devil or Satan? No, it helped make up his mind to betray Jesus to the priests.

Judas "then having received the sop went immediately out" (John 13:30). He went straight to the high priest to make a deal on his payment—thirty pieces of silver. When Judas's evil plan was exposed, his mind and heart changed. He knew he had to do what was in his heart—make some money—even if it meant the death of a friend. In doing so, he became a real Satan or "adversary" to Jesus, a real opposer and enemy to Jesus. The only evil spirit that entered Judas was his own wicked plan to do evil to Jesus. The problem was his own heart, not a supernatural devil.

Remember that the words *Satan* and *devil* both mean "adversary." Jesus did not say that a devil was the cause of His death. He laid the blame squarely on Judas himself, and not on a supernatural fallen angel named Satan. "The son of man goeth as it is written of him: But woe unto the man by whom the son of man is betrayed! It had been good for that man if he had not been born" (Matthew 26:24). The evil doing was all about Judas, not a devil from heaven or the pits of hell. Matthew 26:25 says, "Then Judas, which betrayed him, answered and said, Master, is it I? [Jesus] said unto him, Thou has said." In other words, "Yes, it is you." The sin was charged to the man Judas because of his own heart and action. Judas was a devil in the sense of an "adversary" of Jesus.

The word *Satan* is used once again to reveal the heart of man, to describe the evil heart's intent to do evil.[20] "Peter said, Ananias, Why hath Satan filled thine heart to lie to the Holy Ghost, and to keep back part of the price of the land?" The evil heart is revealed in the next verse: "Why hast thou conceived this thing in thine heart?" (Acts. 5:3-4).

About three hours later, Peter asks Sapphira, the wife of Ananias, about her own involvement in Ananias's actions. "Then Peter said unto her, How is it that ye have agreed together to tempt the Spirit of the Lord?" (Acts. 5:9). In this case, Satan was both husband and wife. Ananias lied, from selfish motives and in agreement with his wife, to misrepresent the extent of their property. The Satan filling their hearts was the spirit of flesh. They lusted and lied, and their greed cost them their lives.

Where Does the Devil Live?

We read in the book of James, "But every man is tempted when he is drawn away of his own lust, and enticed. Then when lust hath conceived, it bringeth forth sin, and sin, when it is finished, bringeth forth death." (James1:14–15). Nothing is said about a supernatural being as the problem. The outcome of the war between spirit and flesh is determined by a person's mind—what he thinks, what he desires, and what is in his heart. All sin proceeds from the desires of the flesh, which take root and grow in a person's mind.

A Few Examples

"Out of the Heart proceeds evil thought, murders, adulterers, fornications, thefts, false witness, blasphemies" (Matthew 15:19).

"Because the carnal mind is enmity against God: for it is not subject to the law" (Romans 8:7). Enmity can be understood as hostility, hatred,

---

[20] *Strong's Concordance* H7853, 7854, and G45670.

rejection, or strong animosity. This is the same enmity God placed between Adam's seed and the Serpent seed in the garden (see Genesis 3:15).

"Now the works of the flesh are manifested, which are these: fornication, uncleanness lasciviousness, idolatry, witchcraft, hatred, variance, emulations, wrath, strife, seditions, heresies, envying, murders, drunkenness, reveling and such like" (Galatians 5:19–21).

"For all that is in the world, the lust of the flesh, and the lust of the eyes, and the pride of the life, is not of the father but is of the world" (1 John 2:16). This is what makes one a devil toward God—doing the things mentioned above from the heart and being of the world.

—————— Satan or the Devil in Us ——————

What is the great Satan or adversary, which every man should fear? It is called the spirit of the flesh, and it must be repressed for a man to avoid doing evil.

If a man surrenders to the flesh, he walks in the way of death. Romans 8:13 tells us, "If ye live after the flesh ye shall die, but if ye through the spirit do mortify the deeds of the body, ye shall live." Similarly, we read in Galatians 5:17, "For the flesh lusteth against the Spirit and the Spirit against the flesh and these are contrary the one to the other: So that ye cannot do the things that ye would." In other words, get your mind under control.

All the scriptures we have read suggest that to rid oneself of the devil is to *not* do the things mentioned and to mortify—to destroy, subdue, or deaden the appetite to partake. This is explained in Ephesians 4:17 as not "having the understanding darkened, being alienated from the life of God through the ignorance that is in them, because of the blindness of their heart." How clear it is, that darkness and ignorance of the true Word of God leave people blind to the reality of the nonexistence of a fallen angel that challenges God and His creation daily.

The hearing of the Word brings forth faith and is the tool needed to create a new man within, who, in the process of time, kills the old man by the renewing of the mind that was hostile toward God.

Who Is the Old Man? Adam or Satan?

"That ye put off concerning the former conversation the old man, which is corrupt according to the deceitful lust" (Ephesians 4:22). The old man is none other than a sinner in darkness and is corrupted by their conversation. The old man seeks those things of the flesh and the world that are enemies of God.

The scripture speaks about a new man in Ephesians 4:24: "And that ye put on the new man, which after God is created in righteousness and true holiness." This is the result of Jesus Christ becoming a part of a person's life (the second Adam).

The old man (Satan) to be destroyed symbolizes the evil and corrupt lifestyle that you lived when you were in darkness before learning about Jesus Christ. To destroy the old man in you, according to Paul, you must "be renewed in the spirit of your mind" (Ephesians 4:23). Paul also said that lying is of the devil and that we should not "give place to the devil" (Ephesians 4:27–31).

Is there anything here about a supernatural fallen angel? No.

In James 4:7, James said, "Submit yourselves therefore to God, Resist the devil and he will flee from you." And we read in Matthew 15:18–20 that "these things are your adversary-Satan, the Devil."

Resist what? The devil that be in you. It is that which is in your heart and mind that becomes an adversary to God. Saying no to evil will rid you of the old man.

What Devil Is James Talking About?

It makes good sense, when you see the truth, resisting the devil is the same as resisting your evil desires and thoughts. If you lust for sex, but you make up your mind not to do evil and say no, you have resisted the devil and he flees from you. He flees because you got your thoughts and heart set on doing the right thing. But if you fail to resist the lust of the flesh (sex, money, and so on) and commit the act against your better judgment, the devil wins.

Satan works with the mind and thought process of the individual regardless of their status in the world, whether Christian or not. Satan will be more visible in people who are ignorant about the Bible and who don't care about learning the truth. People love darkness, and Jesus recognized this in His parable of the Sower.

Neither Jesus' disciples nor the crowds who came to hear Him could understand His parables. "And the disciples came unto him, Why speaketh thou unto them in parables?" (Matthew 13:10). Jesus did not want the people to understand, because His lessons were for the disciples, not the crowd. "He answered and said unto them, because it is given unto you to know the mysteries of the kingdom of heaven, but to them it is not given" (Matthew 13:11). Jesus made no effort to open their eyes.

The Devil of the New Testament

The word *devil* and the tradition of a supernatural evil being; gives way to the biblical doctrine of Satan. The Greek word *devil* was used to refer to slanderers and accusers. If a person was a slander or accuser, they would be considered a devil. "Even so must their wives be grave, not slanderers [devils], sober, faithful in all things" (1 Timothy 3:11). "Without natural affection, trucebreakers, false accusers [devils], incontinent, fierce, despisers of those that are good" (2 Timothy 3:3). "The aged women likewise, that they be in behavior as becoming holiness, not false accusers [devils], not given to much wine, teachers of good things" (Titus 2:3).

Again, the Hebrew word *Satan* is translated as "devil" in Greek. Just as Jesus applied *Satan* to Peter, so He applied *devil* to Judas: "Have not I chosen you twelve, and one of you is a devil!" (John 6:70). Judas's heart made him a devil; he was a betrayer and a false accuser.

In talking about the wives of deacons, Paul says, "Even so must their wives be grave, not slanderers [*diabolos* or devils]" (1 Timothy 3:11). The same standards applied to men: "For men shall be ... without natural affection, truce-breakers, false accuser [*diaboloi*]" (2 Timothy 3:2–3). Finally, as we read in Titus 2:3, "The aged women likewise that they be in behavior as becometh holiness, not false accusers [diabolos]."

Jesus applied the term *devil* to the persecuting authorities of the Roman state. He said in His letter to John, and to the church at Smyrna, "The devil shall cast some of you into prison" (Revelation 2:10).

Who Was This Devil?

The people who killed the Christians had rejected the new religion and desired to have no part of it. Even being associated with Christians could cost people their lives; so many people wanted the preachers to just leave them alone. Their religion was just fine as it was.

In Hebrews 2:14, we read as follows: "Forasmuch then as the children are partakers of flesh and blood, he [Jesus] also himself likewise took part of the same, that through death he might destroy him that had the power of death that is the devil." Who is the "him"? Who has the power of death? "But every man is tempted when he is drawn away of his own lust, and enticed. Then when lust hath conceived, it bringeth forth sin, and sin, when it is finished, bringeth forth Death." (James1:14-15).

Paul said, "Forasmuch then as the children are partakers of flesh and blood, he also himself likewise took part of the same; that through death He might destroy him that had the power of death, that is, the devil; and deliver them who through fear of death were all their lifetime subject to bondage" (Hebrews 2:14–16). How can Satan be alive and busier than ever in the work of hunting mortal souls, if Jesus came for the very purpose of destroying him? (To destroy means to kill or put out of existence.[21])

The *he* referred to above, in Hebrews 2:14, is sin, the author of death, the devil. Strange as it may seem, the devil in which so many churches believe has the "power of death"! Where did he get all this power to take people's lives and destroy them by death? The devil must act as God's agent and do His dirty work. After all, it is God who punishes people for infractions of divine law, as in the case of Adam.

It is God who says to Moses, "See now that I, even I am He, and there is no god with me: I kill, and I make alive, I wound, and I heal: neither is there any that can deliver out of my hand" (Deuteronomy 32:39). God,

---

[21] *Webster's Ninth New Collegiate Dictionary*, s.v. "destroy."

and not the devil, reigns in absolute authority. God dispenses retribution and enforces His own law, not a hostile archangel presumed to be at eternal enmity with him.

John says, "For this purpose the Son of God was manifested, that he might destroy the works of the devil" (1 John 3:8). Did Jesus affect the purpose of His manifestation? If so—and who will deny it?—is it not reasonable to believe that Jesus came and did as He said, to accomplish the overturn of all that is done by the Bible's devil? Did Jesus not destroy all Satan's works, or was it only part of Satan works? If so, the Bible devil is dead. For Christ has come in the flesh to destroy the devil and all his works, but there is no devil of the supernatural order.

What Did Christ Accomplish in His Death?

The devil Christ has come to destroy is sin. Let us consider Paul's words quoted above. Paul expounds on the reason why Jesus came, and that Christians should not be concerned with the sin that is called the devil, which causes death. Sin separates man from God. Jesus came and removed the veil that separated the people and the Creator, and broke down walls to open the door for the salvation of mankind.

One of the things that Jesus came to do is recorded in Hebrews 9:26: "For then must he often have suffered since the foundation of the world: but now once in the end of the world hath he appeared to "put away sin" by the sacrifice of himself." How? By his death. Jesus came to put away "sin" which is the devil that has the power of death. Sin in people's lives is the devil that Jesus came to destroy. This has nothing to do with any supernatural being.

In 1 Corinthians 15:3, this is Paul's message: "For I delivered unto you first of all that which I also received, how that Christ died for our sins according to the scripture." Paul mentions nothing except the sin that Christ came and died for. Christ's death alone can rid a person of their internal devils. Sin is rooted deep within the individual's own heart and desires.

In Isaiah 53:5, we read that Jesus came to be our healer: "But he was wounded for our transgressions; he was bruised for our iniquities:

the chastisement of our peace was upon him, and with his stripes we are healed." Note: This has nothing to do with your physical healing, but only ones spiritual healing.

First Peter 2:24 says, "Who his own self bare our sins in his own body on the Tree that we being dead to sins, should live unto righteousness: by whose stripes ye were healed." Again, this refers not to a body healing, but to a spirit healing. A new man is created through Christ's mission.

"And ye know that he [Jesus] was manifested to take away our sins, and in him is no sin" (1 John 3:5). He tells us not to continue to live with our sin every day, but to go and sin no more. As Jesus told the woman engaged in adultery, if you know what sin is and do it, you are of the devil. However, if you know what sin is and do not do it, you become sons of God. Sin is an individual choice. "I set before you life and good, and death and evil" (Deuteronomy 30:15). To sin is death, but to not sin is life. Choose life.

What Does All This Mean?

Christ's death destroyed and took out of the way "the sin of the world." Jesus destroyed the Bible's devil, but not the popular devil of the average church doctrine of today. Most churches today teach and believe, for the most part, that Satan is still at large, but that he is acting in his own person, as a representative man.

"For what the law could not do, in that it was weak through the flesh, God sending his own Son in the likeness of sinful flesh, and for sin, condemned sin in the flesh" (Romans 8:3). Sin in the flesh, then, is the devil destroyed by Jesus in his death. This is the devil having the power of death, for it is sin—and nothing else but sin—that causes men to die. Adam learned this, and on the day he disobeyed and sinned, he died. Sin is the problem, and it brings death. In Hebrews 2:14, Paul refers to "him who had the power of death, that is, the devil." And Romans 5:12 tells us, "Wherefore, as by one man sin entered into the world and DEATH by sin, and so DEATH passed upon all men, for all have sinned."

── What Brought Death Into the World? ──

In 1 Corinthians 15:21, Paul is rather clear on this subject: "For since by man came death, by man came also the resurrection of the dead." By man—not by a supernatural devil that fell from heaven.

── What Is the Cost of Sin? ──

Paul said in Romans 6:23, "For the wages of Sin is death. But the gift of God is eternal life through Jesus Christ our Lord." Wages are what you earn, sin is what you did, and death is the result. "Then when lust hath conceived, it bringeth forth sin: and sin, when it is finished, bringeth forth [spiritual] death" (James 1:15).

Jesus came to destroy sin (the devil) that reveals itself from within the heart of every person. Death was decreed in the Garden of Eden by God, as the consequence of Adam's transgression.

── What Did James Say About This? ──

James draws our attention to that which is found within man: "But every man is tempted, when he is drawn away of his own lust, and enticed. Then when lust hath conceived, it bringeth forth sin: and sin, when it is finished, bringeth forth death" (James 1:14–15). Paul said he found "another law in my members, warning against the law of my mind" (Romans 7:23). In 1 John 2:16, we read, "For all that is in the world, the lust of the flesh, and the lust of the eye, and the pride of life, is not of the Father, but is of the world."

The god of this world is Satan, who represents lust for the things of the world. When a man see the light through the knowledge of the truth, and is made aware of God's will in his mind and the nature of his actions, a new law is introduced. This is the Spirit, evolved by the Spirit, through inspired men of God.

When a Person Says He Is Filled with the Spirit, What Is He Saying?

Does this mean he has a ghost or a spirit from heaven in him? How does he get the Spirit? Look at what Jesus said: "It is the spirit that quickeneth, the flesh profiteth nothing; the words that I speak unto you, they are spirit, and they are life" (John 6:63). Words spoken are not visible, and thus they are spirit in that sense.

The warfare established in a man's nature by the introduction of the truth is warfare of the two principles. First, the desire of the flesh: lust of the flesh, lust of the eye, and pride of life. And second, the commandments of the Spirit. Here's how Paul describes this: "For the flesh lusteth against the spirit, and the spirit against the flesh and these are contrary the one to the other: so that ye cannot do the things that ye would" (Galatians 5:17). It's an individual choice. If you choose the flesh, you die. If you are filled with the living Word of God, you live.

Paul says that to be filled with the Spirit is to be filled or enlightened in the Word, and to win the war between right and wrong, the Spirit and flesh. Then you defeat the devil and Satan of your life, by the renewing of your mind. When you think of something, good or bad, how do you react toward those thoughts?

To be contrary means to be in conflict with the opposite, or unfavorable to each other.[22] Why is there a war between the flesh and the spirit? You have the knowledge of good and evil and you know the rewards of each. The war is making the choice that leads to life or death, flesh or Spirit.

How Do You Win This War?

In Galatians 5:16, Paul says, "This I say then, walk in the Spirit, and ye shall not fulfill the lust of the flesh." And again, in Romans 6:12 "Let not sin therefore reign in your mortal body, that ye should obey it in the lust thereof." That should be your thinking and your action.

Paul is saying that you, and only you, can cast out the devil, which

---

[22] *Webster's Ninth New Collegiate Dictionary*, s.v. "contrary."

is sin in the form of lust of the flesh and pride of life. Despite what your flesh desires, your mind knows what is lawful and not lawful before God. Paul is saying that you are your own worst enemy, and the battle is to get yourself under control. Paul mentions nothing about a supernatural devil causing problems for you:

> For they that are after the fleshes do mind the things of the flesh; but they that are after the Spirit, the things of the Spirit; or to be carnally minded is death, but to be spiritually minded is life and peace. Because the carnal mind is enmity [hostile] against God: for it is not subject to the law of God, neither indeed can be So then they that are in the flesh cannot please God. But ye are not in the flesh, but in the Spirit, if so be that the Spirit of God dwell in you. Now if any man has not the Spirit of Christ, he is none of his Therefore, brethren, we are debtors, not to the flesh, to live after the flesh. For if ye live after the flesh, ye shall die: but if ye through the Spirit do mortify [put to death] the deeds of the body, ye shall live. (Romans 8:5–9, 12–13)

To walk in the Spirit is to have your mind filled with the word of God. Did not Jesus say in John 6:63, "The words that I speak unto you, they are spirit, and they are life." It is a choice. His words are life. How important is it to be filled with the Spirit (Word) that will give you life? If you are empty headed, you have no Word (Spirit life) in your mind; your carnal mind is ruling and thus you will die.

In 1 John 3:8, we read that "He that committeth sin is of the devil." Why should such a matter be obscured by personification? "If ye were of the world, the world would love his own" (John 15:19). Things are personified in the Word of God, using the gendered language of Greek and Hebrew.

Riches

Matthew 6:24 says, "No man can serve two masters: for either he will hate the one, and love the other ... Ye cannot serve God and mammon." Material things are opposed to things of God.

Sin

"Jesus answered them, Verily, verily, I say unto you; whosoever committeth sin is the servant of sin" (John 8:34). "Sin hath reigned unto death" (Romans 5:21). Sin is the equivalent of a servant of Satan or the devil. "Know ye not, that to whom ye yield yourselves servants to obey, his servants ye are to whom ye obey, whether of sin unto death, or of obedience unto righteousness? ... Being then made free from sin, ye become the servants of righteousness." (Romans 6:16, 18).

The Spirit as Male Gender

John 16:13 says, "When he, the Spirit of truth is come, he will guide you into all truth: for he shall not speak of himself." Who is *he*? He is the Spirit of truth, which will set you free.

Wisdom as Female Gender

"Happy is the man that findeth wisdom, and the man that getteth understanding [knowledge] ... She [wisdom] is more precious than rubies: and all the things thou canst desire are not to be compared unto her" (Proverbs 3:13, 15).

Wisdom is defined as "knowledge, the ability to discern inner qualities, good judgment sense, a wise attitude or course of action."[23] The word *wisdom* was personified by assigning it the female gender, a process that happens frequently in the Bible. For example, Proverbs 9:1 says, "Wisdom hath builded her house, she hath hewn out her seven pillars."

— The Nation of Israel as a Young Lady —

"Again I will build thee, and thou shalt be built, O virgin of Israel: thou shalt again be adorned with thy tabrets" (Jeremiah 31:4).

"I have surely heard Ephraim bemoaning himself thus; thou hast chastised me, and I was chastised, as a bullock unaccustomed to the yoke: turn thou me, and I shall be turned; for thou art the Lord my God" (Jeremiah 31:18).

- The Family of Christ: Christian Believers -

Ephesians 4:13 says, "Till we all come in the unity of the faith, and of the knowledge of the Son of God, unto a perfect man." All believers are considered as one man, all the saints of God are considered as one perfect man, and all things are common in agreement. In Ephesians 4:4, Paul says, "There is one body." And again in 1 Corinthians 12:27, Paul personifies all the follows of Christ: "Ye are the body of Christ."

We read in Ephesians 5:23 that "Christ is the head of the church [people] and he is the savior of the body [believers]." And Paul says in Colossians that Christ "is the head of the body, the church ... I fill up that which is behind of the affliction of Christ in my flesh for his body's sake, which is the church" (Colossians 1:18, 24).

---

[23] *Webster's Ninth New Collegiate Dictionary*, s.v. "wisdom."

"I have espoused you to one husband that I may present you as a chaste virgin to Christ" (2 Corinthians 11:2). In this passage, Paul is telling us that the total church body of believers was considered as one chaste virgin to Christ, the husband. "Let us be glad and rejoice, and give honor to him: for the marriage of the lamb [Christ] is come, and his wife [church of believers] hath made herself ready" (Revelation 19:7).

New State of Mind Developed in the Truth

Colossians 3:9 says, "Ye have put off the old man with his deeds." This old man represents the evil in your life before Christ comes in. The old man is truly a man of the world. "That ye put off concerning the former conversation the Old man, which is corrupt according to the deceitful lusts. And that ye put on the new man, which after God is created in righteousness and true holiness." (Ephesians 4:22, 24). To put off or put on is the individual's choice and responsibility.

Some say that the old man is the devil. That being said, the old man—the devil—is dead. Romans 6:6 say, "Knowing this that the old man is crucified (died) with him." This old man was put to rest at the cross when Jesus said, "It is finished" (John 19:30). What was finished? The old man, the devil, was crucified "that the body of sin might be destroyed, that henceforth we should not serve sin" (Romans 6:6). In verse 7, the devil is dead: "For he that is dead is freed from sin." Paul said he died daily, and so must we.

The Spirit of Disobedience

"Wherein in time past ye walked according to the course of this world, according to the prince of the power of the air, the spirit that now worketh in the children of disobedience. Among whom also we all had our conversations in times past in the lust of our flesh, fulfilling the desires of the flesh and of the mind" (Ephesians 2:2–3). What is the prince of the power of the air? It is your own self-will, your Spirit mind. The prince of the air is your thoughts, working for good or bad in your life. "Now is the judgment of this world; now shall the prince of this world be cast out" (John 12:31).

The Bible in every part belongs to the Oriental languages generally, Hebrew and Greek. It is open to abuse, like every other good thing, but its effectiveness is beyond question. Sin is the great slanderer of God, denying His supremacy, wisdom, and goodness.

Eve spent too much time conversing with the adversary, who persuaded her to disobey and caused the downfall of the first family. Who was her adversary? In the words of the Bible; "The serpent was more subtle than any beast of the field which the Lord God had made" (Genesis 3:1).

Satan said to Eve, "Ye shall not surely die: for God doth know that in the day ye eat thereof, then your eyes shall be opened, and ye shall be as gods, knowing good and evil" (Genesis 3:4–5). Why did God not want Adam and Eve to know good and evil? God did not tell them what would happen, except that they would die. Knowing the difference between good and evil right and wrong, means, that we are held accountable. We cannot do wrong and get away with it. Adam and Eve needed to learn obedience.

The serpent was a slanderer of God, in affirming that what God had said was not true. The serpent became a devil—and not only a devil, but *the* devil—since he originated the slander, causing our first parents to disobey the divine command. "That old serpent, called the devil and Satan" is the symbolic description of the world in its political totality. As we read in Revelation 11:15, "And the seventh angel sounded; and there were great voices in heaven, saying, the kingdoms of this world are become the kingdom of our Lord, and of his Christ; and he shall reign forever and ever." The fruits are the sins known as the devil's works, which started with a lie and exist today (see Galatians 5:19–21).

The fruits of disobedience are with us today and have produced a generation of human serpents. All evil starts with a person's thought process, and the fruits of their thinking bring forth evil works with which we deal every day in our communities across the world. But this devil of the mind can be controlled.

The Heart Is a Deceiver
and Can Be Your Devil

Knowledge can be defined as a fact or condition of knowing something through experience, or to learn by experience.[24]

- "And deceive not with thy lips" (Proverbs 24:28)
- "Not to deceive thyself" (Jeremiah 37:9)
- "And if the prophet be deceived when he hath spoken a thing, I the Lord have deceived that prophet" (Ezekiel 14:9).
- "The heart is deceitful above all things, and desperately wicked: who can know it?" (Jeremiah 17:9)
- "O Lord, thou hast deceived me, and I was deceived" (Jeremiah 20:7). This is the Lord's doing.
- "But, O Lord of hosts, that triest the righteous, and seest the reins and the heart" (Jeremiah 20:12). All are looked at and proved.
- "And with all deceivableness of unrighteousness in them that perish; because they receive not the love of the truth, that they might be saved. And for this cause God shall send them strong delusion, that they should believe a lie. That they all might be damned who believed not the truth, but had pleasure in unrighteousness" (2 Thessalonians 2:10–12).

Truth is knowledge that can set us free. Truth is knowing Christ, because He is truth. Truth is also the Tree of Life. Jesus could say, "Ye serpents ... how can ye escape the damnation of hell?" (Matthew 23:33), and again, "Ye are of your father the devil [slanderer, serpent], and the lust of your father ye will do." (John 8:44)

---

[24] *Webster's Ninth New Collegiate Dictionary*, s.v. "knowledge."

Who Was the Devil in Matthew 23:13–39? The Religious System

"He was a murderer from the beginning, and abode not in the truth, because there is no truth in him. When he speaketh a lie, he speaketh of his own for he is a liar and the father of it" (John 8:44). He brought death upon mankind by inciting Adam and Eve to disobey.

Christ came to destroy the works of the devil, so why not the personal devil? Because, he is already dead. The pagan customs that we follow came from Rome, starting with King Nero and Babylon, including the names of our months and special days such as Easter, Christmas, and others. Those who started these works are dead, but their works live on.

What About Jesus Being Tempted by the Devil? Does This Not Prove a Supernatural Being?

The temptation of Jesus is supposed to prove the personality and power of the Bible's devil. John 6:70 tells us, "Jesus answered them, have not I chosen you twelve, and one of you is a devil?" Judas was classified as a devil, although he was a flesh-and-blood human. Is it possible that the tempter of Jesus could also have been someone with an evil intent, like Judas?

Forty Days of Temptation and Fasting

In Matthew 4:1, "Then was Jesus led up of the spirit into the wilderness to be tempted of the devil." Could it be that Jesus needed time to get His mind prepared? In that verse, did God and Satan patch things up and get back on good terms? Why did God, through the Holy Spirit, lead Jesus out to be tempted by the devil, unless there was something else in Jesus that needed to be addressed? Maybe it had something to do with obedience: "Though he were a Son, yet learned he obedience by the things which he suffered" (Hebrews 5:8).

Why Did Jesus Have to Suffer?

Jesus was preparing himself to be a sacrifice, and the sacrifice had to be without spot or blemish. Hebrews 5:9 says, "And being made perfect, he became the author of eternal salvation unto all them that obey him." Jesus was physically and mentally prepared to be sacrificed through all the suffering He had encountered prior to the crucifixion. He had been made perfect. "And being found in fashion as a man, he humbled himself, and became obedient unto death, even the death of the cross" (Philippians 2:8).

Luke 4:5–8

What About Taking Jesus to the Pinnacle of the Temple?

In the day of Jesus, you would need a working knowledge of the temple and how it was built, its wall, and its purpose. Without this knowledge, the temple will be a little difficult to explain. However, we only need to understand that the top of the temple was also used by the community to walk about and look at the countryside.

The pinnacle of the temple—as we are informed by Josephus, a Jew—had an elevated court, a place for public walking[25]. On one side, this temple court overlooked the valley of Jehoshaphat, which was two hundred feet deep and thus provided a place to commit suicide—which the tempter ask Jesus to do. This is where the tempter, no doubt, walked with Jesus and proposed that He prove that He was God's son by jumping off the wall, knowing that God would save him. This would surely prove Jesus to be the son of God.

Some people point to Christ's conveyance to a high mountain, where Satan showed Him all the kingdoms of the world in a moment of time. The field of vision was in proportion to the altitude. But taking someone to the top of a mountain does not mean that you physically carry them up. A friend of mine went to the top of Pilot Mountain in North Carolina

---

[25] See Matthew 4:2–11 and Luke 4:5–8.

to view the surrounding area with me, but I didn't physically carry him up the mountain. We went together up the mountain to view the area.

The highest mountain in the area where Jesus and the tempter went up was Mount Zion, which was 2,600 feet high at that time. Presently it measures 531 feet from the base to the top.

All the land that Jesus could see was under the control of Pontius Pilate, the ruler of Jerusalem at that time. Pontius Pilate had the power to give this land to Jesus. The devil with which Jesus had to contend was no doubt an authority in the community of the temple, such as a high priest, who had contact with the government leader. Pilate didn't care about Jesus and His mission. It was the church and the high priest who had a problem with Jesus, and they wanted Him dead, even if they had to try to get Jesus to compromise himself by bowing down to the tempter and submitting to the authority.

Who was this devil? No one can say for sure, but it could have been the high priest in the temple who was threatened by Jesus. As in the case of Job's Satan, we can only be sure about whom he was not. Sometimes God uses people to perform strange acts, like the adversary of Job who created problems for him. God did something like this with Moses, too. In Exodus 4:21, we read, "And the Lord said unto Moses, 'When thou goest to return into Egypt, see that thou do all those wonders before Pharaoh which I have put in thy hand.'" Is this not the same as the case of God giving the adversary (Satan) power to afflict Job? Moses was a human with special powers, like Job's Satan.

Right or wrong, the temptation of Jesus affords no real proof to the popular theory about a supernatural devil, which it is often brought forward to prove. Biblical language and pagan theories are put together and made to fit. The church will go to great lengths to hold to their doctrinal beliefs, even knowing that they are wrong. Over the years, doctrine has been set in stone. The church will not change their position, because to do so would mean admitting that they've been wrong.

What About Demons?

In the Old Testament, the word *devils* are found four times:

1. "And they shall no more offer their sacrifices unto devils" (Leviticus 17:7).
2. "They sacrificed unto devils, not to God" (Deuteronomy 32:17).
3. "And he ordained him priests for the high places, and for the devils and for the calves which he had made" (1 Chronicles 11:15).
4. "Yea they sacrificed their sons and their daughters unto devils" (Psalm 106:37).

Let's look again at Deuteronomy 32:17: "They sacrificed unto devils, not to God, to gods whom they knew not, to new gods that came newly up, whom your fathers feared not." The reason they were not feared was that they were all made by hand with wood and stones. The "devils" sacrificed to by Israel were the idols of the heathen—not supernatural beings, but idols carved to look like goats.

What Were These Devils?

"They were mingled among the heathen, and learned their works: and they served their idols, which were a snare unto them. Yea, they sacrificed their sons and daughters unto devils [idols] and shed innocent blood, even the blood of their sons and of their daughters, whom they sacrificed unto the idols of Canaan" (Psalm 106:35–38). This is a description of a pagan religious practice, like that of Moloch as described in the Bible.

Obviously the idols of Canaan were lifeless blocks of wood and stone. So their designation as "devils" demonstrates that the use of specific words in the Old Testament gives no countenance to the idea that "devils" are personal beings, serving the great devil in his works of mischief and damnation.

In the New Testament, Paul's use of the word, in the same way that it is used in the Old Testament, suggests that he ignored the pagan view of the matter. "But I say, that the things which the Gentiles sacrifice, they sacrifice to devils, and not to God: and I would not that ye should have fellowship with devils. Ye cannot drink the cup of the Lord, and the cup of devils: ye cannot be partakers of the Lord's Table and of the tables of devils" (1 Corinthians 10:20–21).

Paul repeatedly mentions devils, and *devils* here apply to the idols and gods of pagan superstition. First Corinthians 10:19 says, "What say I, then that the idol is anything, or that which is offered in sacrifice to idols is anything." Paul applies the word *devils* to idols, of which he says, "We know that an idol is nothing in the world" (1 Corinthians 8:4). The word *devils*, as used by Paul, lend no proof to the popular view of Satan as a fallen angel from heaven.

The student of the Bible must understand that *devils* in the original Greek is *diabolos*, In Greek, *devils* is the plural of *daemon*, which has a very different meaning from *diabolos*. Daemon was the name given by the Greeks to spirit beings of imagination, who were thought to exist in the air and to act as mediators between God and man, for good or evil. These imaginary spirits belong to pagan mythology and have no place in the system of truth.

In Isaiah 65:11, we read, "But ye are they that forsake the Lord that forget my holy mountain, that prepare a table for that troop, and that furnish the drink offering unto that number." Here's Isaiah 28:2 from the Hebrew Bible: "Adonai has someone strong and powerful. He comes like a hailstorm, a destructive tempest, like a flood of water; rushing overwhelming with his hands he hurls them to the ground."[26] So from this and the previously cited passage, we understand what is meant in the English translation of Psalms 96:5: "For all the gods of the nations are idols, but the Lord made the heavens." All the gods of the Gentiles are *daimonia* (idols)—not devils, but some powers of imaginary intelligence of material nature. "And they said unto him … It is not because there is not a God in Israel that thou sendest to enquire of Beelzebub the god of Ekron?" (2 Kings 1:16).

Jesus did not condemn their religion, because doing so could have cost Him His life. He did, however, use the name of their god Beelzebub.

---

[26] Stern, David H. *Complete Jewish Bible.*1998 Clarksville MD

In Matthew 17:15–18, a father had a son who was thought to be devil possessed because he was insane. The son was unbalanced at times, which caused him to fall even into the fire, and he was at times out of control. The father tells Jesus in verse 16, "And I brought him to thy disciples, and they could not cure him." Then Jesus rebuked the devil and healed the son of his problem. Matthew doesn't say the child had a devil, but only that he needed healing from being insane—and Jesus rebuked the insanity. The phrase *cast out* is the same as being healed or set free of whatever the problem might be.

What About Devils Being Cast Out in Matthew 12:22?

The man who was brought to Jesus in Matthew 12:22 were called "possessed." But at that time, people didn't know the difference between having a medical problem and being possessed by the devil. Matthew tells us that this man was blind and dumb, and that Jesus healed him so that he could see and hear. Being blind and dumb doesn't suggest involvement by a devil of supernatural origin. The scripture is clear that Jesus healed him: "Then was brought unto Him one possessed with a devil, and blind and dumb and He healed him, insomuch that the blind and dumb both spoke and saw" (Matthew 12:22).

Mark 9:17 records the story of Jesus healing a son with a dumb spirit—another incident that cannot be classified as a devil possession. Because of our advanced medical knowledge, today such stories would not be considered as instances of demon possession. Today, as in Jesus's time, many physical and mental illnesses are actually caused by brain disorders. If we agreed that demons and devils are the cause of deafness or blindness, then we would have to conclude that all sickness is of the devil and all who are sick are devil possessed. Heart problems, cancer, glaucoma, liver problems, kidney failure, diabetes, bowel disorders, schizophrenia, and delusional disorders—all are caused by a demon or devil.

But we cannot say that the blind, deaf, dumb, lame, and insane people whom Jesus healed were possessed by a demon, and then exempt other sicknesses as normal and acceptable. If all sickness was devil or demon related, our churches would be full all the time with people seeking to be set free of the demons and devils that possess them. Instead, we find these people in doctors' offices seeking a pill or a good old shot in the arm. The devil in the needle that takes pain away sometimes fells good!

Today we know that sickness is often related to a family's genetic history. Also, children are sometimes born with problems caused by the mother using drugs or drinking alcohol during pregnancy. Even smoking by a mother can have an effect on their unborn child, or a parent can pass on to their child a blood disease.

Our health is also affected by the environment itself—the air we breathe the food we eat, our physical activity, and our general state of mind. Today many diseases can be cured, and research continues to come up with new cures all the time. We can't yet cure everything, but medical science can and does help many, many people. People who continue to believe that sickness is the work of a demon or devil must be happy to know that we've learned how to cast out the devil that causes headaches with Excedrin tablets.

In Jesus' time, many people believe that only a priest could heal them of the evil spirits or demons that caused them to be sick and even die. Some people went even further and claimed that sin was the root cause of illness. But Jesus declared to the people, concerning the blind man who was healed, that neither the man nor his parents had sinned, but that God would be glorified that day. And today, with our knowledge of medications and drugs, we have set many people free of evil spirits and demons. The truth will surely set us free.

One father told Jesus that his child sometimes would fall into the fire, which caused people to think that he was possessed by a devil. Actually the child was experiencing seizures, which are a response to an abnormal electrical discharge in the brain—and have nothing to do with a devil of supernatural origin. When the brain is irritated, a seizure occurs, and behavior during seizures varies. Seizures can be triggered by a fever, a brain infection, or even an odd smell or taste... Epilepsy is a disease characterized by recurring seizures, which is what happened with this father's son. Epileptic seizures might last one or two minutes—ten to thirty seconds in a child—and the person may lose consciousness. This father's son might have had what is called a complex partial seizure, in which the person may move their arms and legs in strange and purposeless ways and stagger as they move about. Sometimes seizures are caused by a brain tumor or a lack of blood flow to the brain. Regardless of the cause, you can hardly call seizures a work of a demon or a devil of a supernatural order. They are caused by a physical disorder and have nothing to do with the spiritual world.

In the days of Jesus, knowledge of the healing arts was very limited, and only the upper class could afford the few treatments that were available. The priest in the community was the primary source for treatment. People had to be very careful in the practice of mixing herbs and roots to create medicine. Coughing while mixing herbs could cost a woman her life. This practice was considered to be witchcraft and thus was prohibited, which was also the case in England and America. In my medical training, I have learned that the brain is an amazing organ, capable of strange things.

What About the Swine and Devils Being Cast into Them?

Mark 5:12

"And all the devils besought him, saying; Send us into the swine, that we may enter into them" (Mark 5:12). Once again we are dealing with a person who is sick with a brain disorder. Healing or casting out a disease or devil was no problem for Jesus; He was the Son of God and had all power to send the diseased brain into the swine pen. This man's brain was much like that of Charles Manson, who was sometimes Jesus Christ and at other times something else.

The mad man spoke—although not as a supernatural fallen angel in the form of a demon—and Jesus saw his need and healed him. "For the time will come when they will not endure sound doctrine, but after their own lusts shall they heap to themselves teachers, having itching ears; And they shall turn away their ears from the truth, and shall be turned unto fables" (2 Timothy 4:3–4). The doctrines of a supernatural personal devil and the immortality of the soul are all of pagan origin. But when will the church wake up and rid itself of this doctrine, which causes so much confusion? More time could be spent on loving God and doing unto others as you would have them do unto you.

Hebrews' View of Satan

In Hebrew (Judaism), the biblical word *ha-Satan* means "adversary" or "obstacle," or even "the prosecutor." Recognizing that, God is still viewed as the ultimate judge.

In the book of Job, ha-Satan is the title—not the proper name—of an angel submitted to God. He is considered by the Jews as the "divine court's chief prosecutor." In Judaism, ha-Satan is not evil; instead, he points out to God the evil inclinations and actions of humankind. In essence, ha-Satan has no power unless humans do evil things. It is only *after* God points out Job's piety that ha-Satan asks for permission to test Job's faith. Job is then afflicted with loss of family, property, and later his health, but still he stays faithful to God. At the conclusion of this book, God appears in a whirlwind, explaining to all that divine justice is inscrutable with human intellect. In the epilogue, Job's possessions are restored and he has a second family to replace the one that died.

Jews claim that the Hebrew Bible came directly from God. If that be the case, let us stay with it! It's the closest thing to the truth that we will ever find. There is no evidence in the Hebrew Torah, the prophets, or other writings to suggest that God created an evil being. In fact, Isaiah, Job, Ecclesiastes, and Deuteronomy all include passages in which God is credited for creating the good *and* the evil of this world. The Hebrew word for *evil* used above is usually translated as "calamity, disaster, or chaos."

In the Hebrew Bible (Tanakh), we read, "And he showed me Joshua the high priest standing before the angel of the Lord, and ha-Satan standing at his right hand to resist him" (Zechariah 3:1). This reading has been erroneously interpreted by some people to mean Satan, the devil, but such is not the case. The Hebrew Bible views ha-Satan as an angel ministering to the desires of God, acting as chief prosecutor. We must realize that God will use whatever he desires to accomplish His will, be it a jackass under Balaam or Peter's roaster from the henhouse. The will of God will be done.

In Genesis 3:1, the serpent is described as a beast of the field. There is no scripture to support the church's interpretation that this beast is a fallen angel known as Satan.

Isaiah 12:1 says, "How art thou fallen from heaven, O Lucifer, son of the morning?" But the title *Lucifer* has nothing to do with a fallen angel called the devil, but only with a king who ruled like a devil in the land. We can thank Jerome for this confusion.

1. It represented the king of Babylon, who fell from his high position.
2. Lucifer is a Latin word for the planet Venus, the morning star.
3. Lucifer as an angel fallen from heaven is not recorded in any Hebrew text. Nevertheless, it is assumed to be true and accepted by the church as real and very active.

In Job 1:6, we find that the sons of God came together to meet God. Did the scripture say that the sons of God were angels, or just sons of God? Some people believe that the sons of God were in fact angels who chose to be transformed into flesh-and-blood beings and decided to marry the daughters of man. Some people even claim that these sons of God were the angels who were cast out of heaven after the war that destroyed the earth. Others believe these sons are the sons of Shem, Noah's son, and they were the God-fearing family on earth at that time. In any case, it does not prove these sons as supernatural, but human.

In Exodus 4:21–23, the Lord told Moses to tell Pharaoh that the whole nation of Israel is his sons. Nothing is said about these sons being angels from heaven. It's true that Satan was present, but that does not prove a fallen angel any more than Peter being Satan or Judas being a devil. If we used the correct wording in that passage from Exodus, it would sound different. The word *adversary* should be used, because *Satan* makes it erroneously sound like a masculine personal devil. The individual was called an adversary in the original text.

Ezekiel 28 is all about the King of Tyrus—or the Prince of Tyrus, who was King Ithobalus II in 573 BC. Again, does the Bible say he was a fallen angel? No, it does not.

The story in Revelation 12:1–12 says nothing to prove this dragon is Satan, a fallen angel from heaven. The battle John saw while in the Spirit on the Lord's Day depicted things that were to happen shortly and afterward—sometime after John's day, not before Adam and Eve's day. And yet the church says it happened *before* John's day. It amazes me that churches juggle the book of Revelation like a deck of cards.

Revelation 1:1 says, "The revelation of Jesus Christ, which GOD gave unto him, to shew unto servant things which must shortly come to pass; and sent and signified it by angel unto servant John." The word is clear—from God to Jesus Christ to the angel and to John, in that order. God also said "shortly" and "hereafter." So who are we to believe, God or man?

Is there a devil or Satan against whom we fight in our spiritual walk? Yes, but it isn't a supernatural being or angel fallen from heaven. The only unseen spirit with which man will ever deal is in the head that rest on his shoulders. In that head dwells a devil called "thoughts," which produce evil in the heart of an individual.

Satan as Prosecutor

We find again in Revelation 12:10, "And I heard a loud voice saying in heaven, Now is come salvation, and strength, and the kingdom of our God, and the power of his Christ: for the accuser [devil, prosecutor] of the brethren is cast down, which accused [prosecuted] them before our God day and night." John heard the good news of Christ and His victory over the world, and King Nero had been put down.

Define the Word Satan

Satan is only a word, not a supernatural being. The word *Satan* is the definition of the Hebrew words *accuser* and *adversary*, or *enemy*. This is a Satan.[27]

Define the Word Devil

The word *devil* is Greek, meaning a "false accuser" or "slanderer" (*diabolos*). The words *Satan, devil, dragon, and serpent* are all representative of a person's character. The things that young people learn are what they are taught at home and abroad, helps build character.

---

[27] *Strong's Concordance.*

If Satan the Devil Is Not Real, —— Explain Satan Cast Out of Heaven —— to Earth as in Revelation 12:9

John says in Revelation 1:10, "I was in the spirit": and none of these things had happened yet. Again, in Revelation 1:1, he said it was to come to pass "shortly." The accuser, the devil in heaven, will fight and be cast out in the future, when he will make war against the saints of God, a war between good and the bad—not where God is, but here in high places on earth.

We create gods and devils to our own liking. We need someone to credit or blame for the good and bad that happens to us. If all is good, the good god has blessed us. But if bad things happen to us, it is the bad god, Satan the devil. So we blame either God of heaven or Satan on earth. It's strange, but true, that many people perceive the problems they incur in this life as all caused by the existence of a fallen devil who is warring against God and His people every day.

—————— The God of Creation Is One ——————

The Father, creator of the heavens and earth, is in control of all things and will not allow anything to be unless He desires or purposes it to be. God rules in the heavens and earth. This is what God said that He did in Deuteronomy 32:39: "See now that I, even I, am he, and there is no god with me. I kill, and I make alive, I wound, and I heal: neither is there any can deliver out of my hand." Notice that He is one God, alone.

This is the God of Creation, who is absolute and immortal with no competition. All power is ordained by God and nothing can change that fact. The Creator can and will do as He pleases. Here are some examples:

(1) "And Moses said thus saith the Lord, about midnight will I go out into the midst of Egypt and all the firstborn in the land shall die" (Exodus 11:4). God Himself or His angel, not a fallen supernatural being, was to kill all the firstborn.

Who Was Going Through Egypt to Kill the Firstborn?

(2) The Lord said, "For I will pass through the land of Egypt this night and will smite all the firstborn in the land of Egypt, both man and beast; and against all the gods of Egypt I will execute judgment. I am the Lord" (Exodus 12:12).

(3) "For the Lord will pass through to smite the Egyptians … And it came to pass, that at midnight the Lord smote all the firstborn in the land of Egypt" (Exodus 12:23, 29). If the Lord comes after you for disobedience, you cannot hide. He killed the firstborn children while they slept. (There is no fallen angel in this action, but the Lord was a "Satan" to Egypt.)

(4) "And the anger of the Lord was kindle against Uzzah; and the Lord God smote him there for his error; and he died by the Art of God" (2 Samuel 6:7). This was no fallen angel, but a supernatural God. We could say that this does prove a supernatural devil, if we point to God as Uzzah's adversary and devil—which He was. God is playing the role of a Satan to the people of Egypt and Uzzah.

(5) Another example of how God deals with disobedience is found in 1 Kings 13:23–24. In this example, God used a lion to kill a disobedient preacher, who was a prophet or priest. Only God the Creator has the power of life and death, not a fallen angel as some believe. We are God's creation and He will not lose control nor give it up to another.

(6) Another example of how God is in control of all situations, whether good or bad, is found in Numbers 22:26–30. The Lord's anger was against Balaam and He was going to kill Balaam, and the angel stood in a narrow place, in the way. The Lord again was in control of this situation by using an angel.

Notice that it was the angel of the Lord who was going to kill Balaam, not a fallen devil from heaven. All these deaths were caused by disobedience to God. People in their churches; talk about their sicknesses, and their troubles, and how the devil is fighting them. Actually it might not be a devil, but the very God whom they serve, chastising them.

As seekers of truth, we trust the Word of God to guide us in all truth, so we may share our knowledge with each other. The Word is clear that our everyday problems are not caused by a fallen devil or Satan from heaven, but by the evil that reveals itself through each of us.

Our intent is to help the reader search for and find the answers for themselves, and make their own decision on the subject from what they have learned by looking at things differently from the traditional views. My hope is that this work will give light and understanding to the student and seeker of the truth.

The traditional view of a personal devil may work best for you. This is what is taught today in most traditional churches and Christian schools. If good things come your way, it must be God. And if bad things happen to you, it must be the devil—or it could be God.

It is a shame to blame God or a devil for the good and bad in our lives, when our life is determined by our own choices, whether good or bad. It is so easy to blame someone other than ourselves. Each and every one of us will stand before the Lord and give an account of our deeds. It will not be a supernatural fallen angel called the devil who will be tried, but the individual themselves. As Romans 14:19 tells us, "We shall all stand before the judgment seat of Christ."

If Satan Is Not a Supernatural Being, Why Did Paul Say This?

"Put on the armor of God that ye may be able to stand against the wiles of the devil" (Ephesians 6:11). Paul says we are supposed to stand against Satan. Let us look at these scriptures and see what we are to stand against and what we should use as armor. What we are to stand against is recorded in Ephesians 6:11–12. Let's look at each word so that we may have a good understanding of Paul's statement:[28]

- Verse 11: *Wiles* means to lure, trick, deceive, or entice.
- Verse 12: *Principalities* refers to an office of authority, as a prince, hierarchy. All this represents people in high places.

---

[28] *The American Heritage College Dictionary*, 3rd ed., s.vv. "wiles," "principalities," "powers," "rulers," "spiritual."

- Verse 12: *Powers* are systems that control or have power to control (government).
- Verse 12: *Rulers* of the darkness of this world are enemies of God at the state level or in church government.
- Verse 12: *Spiritual* weakness in high places refers to religious systems.

This list belongs to a world system with a corrupt state and religious system, not a supernatural angel from heaven called Satan. I believe the corrupt governments on earth will collapse.

How Do We Fight It?

The armor of God is listed in Ephesians 6:14–18:

- Verse 14   "Truth"—Trust the words of Jesus.
- Verse 14   "Breastplate of Righteousness"—Treat people rightly.
- Verse 15   "Feet shod"—Keep preaching the gospel of peace.
- Verse 16   "Shield of faith"—Know the Word.
- Verse 17   "Helmet of Salvation"—Keep your testimony.
- Verse 17   "Sword of the Spirit"—Use the Word.
- Verse 18   "Prayer and supplication in the Spirit"—Keep praying always.

There is no mention of Paul having problems with a fallen angel. His problems were with the local authority and the different groups of religious leaders. He tried to warn them all to beware of certain people who withstood him and hindered his work. This was true of the priest of the old order. The Temple leaders did not like Jesus or the follows of Christ. For the most part the leaders were adversaries or devils toward Jesus and his followers. The leaders of that day did not like changes in their religious beliefs. They like the law and Moses and the control of people.

Resource Helps

Concordance	G = Greek	H = Hebrew
Satan	G4567	H7854
Devil	G1228	H8163, H7700
Devils	G1140	
Evil Spirit	G1142	
Serpent	G3789	H5175, H5172
Slander	G1223	
Barak = Curse	4.1288 = Kneel, Bless	
Face: ----	H6440 Paniym	

Strong's Concordance is a help in determining the true meaning of these words from the Greek and the Hebrew. This will save time when looking up certain words to reinforce the subject discussed. I would always recommend to the reader and students of the Bible to have on hand a good concordance, a good dictionary, and a good reference Bible. It would be good to learn some Greek and Hebrew words and get knowledgeable about key words related to the subject at hand.

The use of the word Tyrus is also used as the word Tyre and Tzor, name of a city

Part Two: Cherubim

Are they angels?

Satan was an anointed cherub.

Will this prove Satan to be a supernatural angel fallen from heaven?

Some people believe that a cherub is a bronze craft used to transport people and God through the universe, and other people believe that cherubim are heavenly angels or beings. It is surprising to learn that the cherub is neither of the above. In this study we hope to learn the mystery of the cherubim of the Bible.

Cherubim

What Are They and Are They Real?

In this section we will delve deeper into the spiritual meaning related to the cherubim of Ezekiel 28. In the Bible, cherubim are an order of celestial beings or symbolic representations. The cherubim, also known as swirlers, discern and execute the will of God with the speed of light, as messengers representing divine wisdom. They also serve as God's chariot and guard the Tree of Life with a flaming sword.

Only those who are holy and perfect may enter where God reigns in man, that being the mind of man. What a man thinks has the same effect and results of that which was thought of in the Garden of Eden. [Life or Death] The thoughts of an individual have the power to bring one closer to God or drive him further away. Thoughts are unseen words that have not been activated. The Hebrew ark was surmounted by cherubim, symbolic of the power and protection of God and the union of the heavenly with the earthly. The name cherubim—*krubh* in Hebrew—appears to be borrowed from the Sumerian *karubu*, a title of Ea.

In this section, we will attempt to define what a cherub really is. Some say cherubim are the angels of the Lord, or angels that minister the will of God. Angels are spirits, which can be earthly as well as heavenly. *Webster's* defines angel as "a spiritual being, an attendant spirit or guardian, messenger."[29]

There are some very interesting notes in *Strong's Concordance* on the subject of cherubim and angels. In Hebrew, cherub is defined as follows:

- "Khaw-rab" (prime root of cherub): to parch through drought; to desolate, destroy, kill, slay, lay waste. (2717)

---

[29] *Webster's Ninth New Collegiate Dictionary*, s.v. "angel."1983 Merriam-Webster, Springfield, Massachusetts

- "Khar-ab" (charab in Chaldean): to demolish or destroy. (2718)
- "kheh'-reb" (chereb): a cutting instrument, as a knife, sword, sharp implement, axe, dagger, or mattock. (2719)
- "Khew-rabe" (chareb): parched or ruined; desolate, dry, waste. (2720)

There is no doubt that a cherub's main function is to kill, destroy, slay, demolish, parch, and lay waste. However, there is not one word mentioned about cherubim being angels or messengers of the Lord. The word *angel* does not appear in any definition of *cherub*. How strange!

In English, an angel is thought of as a spirit being from heaven, but that it is not the case in Hebrew, where the root word is *malak*.[30] The root means "to dispatch as a deputy," but it also can mean "a prophet, priest, teacher, ambassador, angel, or king." *Malakh* means "to send," as a messenger. *Malach* can be "a wind, person, or spiritual force."

Some Jewish rabbis believe that when you perform a commandment, you create an angel that accompanies and influences you, thus creating a proportional spiritual and intellectual connection between you and God. This then becomes a "guardian angel" whose job is to protect and help guide you.

The first mention of cherubim is in Genesis 3:24: "So [God] drove out the man; and [God] placed at the east of the Garden of Eden, and a flaming sword which turned every way, to keep the way of the tree of life." Many people believe that cherubim are angels, but that's not necessarily true. Genesis 3:24 gives us a clue about what cherubim do:

1. They keep the way of the Tree of Life.
2. They turn every way with a flaming sword.

After man was cast out of the garden because of his sin, there had to be a way to stop him from returning. Should man enter the garden in a sin state, he would live as an immortal being, so he had to be restricted from the garden.

By placing man outside the garden, God's riches of truth are hidden

---

[30] *Strong's Concordance* 397, 4399.

and given only to those who understand His mysteries. The Word of God is concealed from the wise and prudent of the world, and only those in Christ can know the secret and mysteries of His truth. God's face-to-face interaction with us ended when man lost his paradise. Now His written Word tells us how we may find our way back home from whence we came, through Jesus the Christ.

"Search the scripture; for in them ye think ye have eternal life: and they are they which testify of me" (John 5:39). Interestingly, the Bible itself testifies that man lost his ability to see and hear God. Otherwise why would we need the written Word or His letters? If God was having communion with us, why would we need the Bible? The Bible is His letter to us, and letters are written when people are separated from each other.

When Jesus came into the world, people failed to grasp that He was the way—and they refused the way. Man is not interested in going home, because of his love for the world. Our carnal minds are focused on the letter, rather than on the man of whom the letter speaks.

When the Spirit opens the Bible's gate, a flood of revelation emerges. What was hidden beyond our imagination—Eden, the garden of God—is seen once again. Our thirst and hunger for communion with the Creator is renewed, as we behold the Tree of Life standing in the midst of the garden. The Bible comes alive as our eyes are fixed upon the glory of the Tree of Life, but looking into it does not mean we possess its gold. God made sure of that when He placed the covering cherubim at its entrance, preventing entry to anything less than the image of Christ. These wings were sown into the Bible's very fabric, especially in the uncountable translation errors that all Bibles contain. The cherubim also had a flaming sword that turns in every direction. If we consult the original Hebrew and Greek texts, we might find our way back to Eden. Remember, the Bible is God's letter to man and the fire of the letter can yet be present, cutting to pieces and burning any flesh that comes near. These cherubim were set for the purpose of guarding and denying access to the Tree of Life. It is impossible for man to return to Eden without a change, but the Word of God changes lives.

Jesus rejoiced at the thought that not just anyone can enter: "In that hour Jesus rejoiced in spirit, and said, I thank thee, O Father, Lord of heaven and earth, that thou hast hid these things from the wise and prudent, and hast revealed them unto babes: even so Father, for so it seems good in thy sight" (Luke 10:21). Is it not a good thing that the riches of His kingdom are not scattered to be trampled under the feet of the unrepentant and unregenerate Adams of the world? These sacred things are reserved for members of His family, who know the mysteries of the kingdom.

"Hearken, my beloved breather, Hath not God chosen the poor of the world rich in faith, and heirs of the kingdom which hath promised to them that love him?" (James 2:5) There is no way for anyone who lives outside of Jesus the Christ to ever understand the simplest of these unsearchable riches.

Romans 11:33 proclaims, "O the depth of the riches both of the wisdom and knowledge of God! How unsearchable are judgments, and ways past finding out!" Searching through all the Bibles in the world will not bring us any closer to the knowledge of the truth. Adam—all people—today must be baptized into Christ, who is the truth; otherwise the cherubim and the flaming sword will prevent us from entry.

The cherubim are creatures of the heavens; in their realm of dominion, they are dreadful and carry tremendous authority. The Hebrew word for cherubim, *keruwbim*, is not clearly understood even by Hebrew scholars. We can get a glimpse of what a cherub is by looking into *Strong's Concordance*. With the spirit of revelation, the windows of heaven will begin to open.

A word is transliterated when one or two letters are changed to make it look and sound like a new language. We get the word *cherub* from the Hebrew *keruwb*, a transliteration of *keruwg*. *Strong's Concordance* tells us that cherubim are imaginary figures." This is true. Cherubim are imaginary beings, images in the mind and lacking substance. In essence, cherubim are imaginings, shadows, figments, and figures of the truth. These imaginary figures have wings and were seen by Ezekiel in the heavens. People who study spiritual things realize that the heavens are not *above* our heads, but *in* our heads. These winged creatures are within and not without. From the heavens of the mind come thoughts, winging their way into our lives. They take shape as intangible imaginations.

These images can be from God or from man, for all things originate in the mind before they are seen in the world. This process can be seen in Genesis 1:26: "And God said, let us make man in our image, after our likeness," in our imagination, according to our thoughts. "So God created man in his own image, in the image of God created he him; male and female created he them." (Genesis 1:27). Thoughts are invisible, but they become very real when spoken from the heaven of our mind.

We need to look closely at the Hebrew root of the English word *image* (iselem), which is close enough to be synonymous with *kerub,* the Hebrew word for cherub.[31] The root meaning of *iselem* (image) is "a shade, phantom, illusion, resemblance, or reprehensive figure." Man, in the image of God, was a shade, a phantom, a thought, an imagination of God that was eventually given form. Man is like God, because he came out of God, so we have the same ability to imagine cherubim. All of man's creations—boats, cars, radios, and so on—started with a thought, an imagination or dream in the mind. Our imaginings become reality only when acted upon.

The Tree of Life is protected by the cherubim. The Bible has protection also, which can be seen in the Gospel of John, although few understand it. "Search the scripture; for in them ye think ye have eternal life: and they are which testify of me. And ye will not come to me, that ye might have life" (John 5:39–40). From the days of Christ until today, many people have believed that as a result of their spiritual beliefs (dogma), they are on their way into the garden where the Tree of Life can be found with its fruits. Many people have read God's letter, but seldom do they come to the knowledge of the truth, which can only be discerned spiritually.

Second Timothy 3:7 speaks of people who are "ever learning and never able to come to the knowledge of the truth." Studying the scripture, and what we imagine of the scripture, will not show us the way, the truth, or the life we seek. Jesus is the way, the truth, and the life. The scripture testifies of Him, but those letters never were—and never will be—that life. There are untold riches in Eden's garden, as detailed in the Bible, but they are of no spiritual worth until they become reality in our own lives. Cherubim (imaginations) are placed there to protect it, until Christ makes the way. If our Bibles translated the Hebrew and Greek accurately, they would not remove the cherubim or the flaming sword, which would still be present in our minds. Without the anointing of Christ, our Bibles would still be the letter that kills. The Spirit of the Word that is written, the watchful cherubim and the flaming sword, prevent the invasion of the natural eye or the carnal mind.

---

[31] *Strong's Concordance* Hebrew 6754–6755.

We must be born from above to even see the kingdom of God. "Except a man be born [from above] again, he cannot see the kingdom of God" (John 3:3). Jesus is the door, and you must go through that door to find the gold, the mysteries of the kingdom. The written word and law put Jesus in the garden tomb and concealed him. The law was carved in stone. But when that stone is removed, as the stone at Jesus' sepulcher was removed, the Lord will be seen rising out of the tomb of carnal reasoning, free of the binding grave clothes of human logic.

Paul had this to say about these stones: "Forasmuch as ye are manifestly declared to be epistle of Christ ministered by us, written not with ink, but with the Spirit of the living God; not in tables of stone, but in fleshly tables of the heart" (2 Corinthians 3:3). When the Lord's Spirit writes upon our hearts, we see and manifest Him, but as long as the stone heart remains, the law is written and Christ will remain obscured. We remain in the tomb. Until the resurrected Christ is seen standing in the garden of tombs, we will be in darkness and void of life. When the stone is removed, the way of life comes forth in victory. He will come alive and rise out of the scripture—alive. Jesus will no longer be a lifeless imagining in men's minds. Christ will not be a letter without substance that renders death, but an ascended reality in our heavens [mind] that give life. We will not seek Him among the dead (law), but among the living, in the heavens within, and we shall find Him alive.

The letter of the law is dead and kills, as we see in 2 Corinthians 3:6: "For the letter killeth, but he Spirit giveth life." If your mind is not spiritual, you will never find your way back into the garden of the Lord.

The first Adam died in Eden, the garden of life, and took creation to the grave with him. But the last Adam rose up alive in the garden of death, and took the creation back to the Father with Him. The first Adam destroyed life, and the last Adam destroyed death.

"For the word of God is quick, and powerful, and sharper than any two-edged sword, piercing even to the dividing asunder of soul and spirit, and of the joints and marrow, and is a discerner of the thoughts and intents of the heart. Neither is there any creature that is not manifested in sight: But all things are naked and opened unto the eyes of him with whom we have to do" (Hebrews 4:12–13). The letter of the law conceals God's truth, and the living Word reveals it. All things are laid open and bare. There are two swords: (1) the sword of the Spirit, and (2) the sword of the flesh. There is a word that quickens and a word that kills. The quickened word reveals the void that lies deep in the fleshly heart of man, and the uninspired word conceals the paradise of God in man.

We recall from the book of Genesis that God placed at the entrance of the garden a cherubim and a flaming sword, to protect the way to the Tree of Life and prohibit anyone from entering. Both the cherubim and a flaming sword were there. That flaming sword is believed by some people to be the living Word of God; however, the sword speaks of *a* word, but not *the* living Word. The Word of God is quick (living) and powerful, revealing what is in man. The sword at the east of the garden conceals the good and evil in man, looking to self (soul) for solution to his problems and finding his way back to the garden (paradise). This path will not lead to the garden; only through Christ can it be found.

The letter of the Word ministers death and darkens our way, and Christ, the living Word, minister's life and provides light for the way. God, through Christ, gave us the light. "For thou hast delivered my soul from death: wilt not thou deliver my feet from falling, that I may walk before God in the light of the living" (Psalm 56:13). And in Psalm 119:105, we read, "Thy word is a lamp unto my feet, and a light unto my path."

The flaming sword that keeps and hedges the Tree of Life does not give life. There is no life in the flaming sword, only death. It represents a law that is rooted in the do's and don'ts of the carnal man. The sword will give direction, not life. The sword is the ministration of death, and anyone who approaches it will die. The main purpose of the cherubim and the flaming sword was to keep man away from life. The word gave death, not life; neither did it lead to life. The sword of death was a word of death. It was not the sword of the Spirit, but a sword of the letter of the word.

The law—the flaming sword—is not the way to God. It does not point, guide, or lead to life, but it bars the sinner from coming to God with its do's and don'ts that kill. The law and its words have not saved a single soul of Adam's fallen race. Churches around the world have polluted themselves with a form of truth, while empty ceremonies, ordinances, and rituals have held deadly sway.

The flaming sword of the dead letter of the Word has cut its way from pulpits until the precious life of the Spirit has been lost, and the stench of death hangs like a shroud over God's people. Man-made rules and rituals of the church hang to the law, but its word is a dead word and will kill you. The living Word will cause you to live. It will cut away the cherubim (imaginations) that fly through the heavens of your mind. It is living, powerful, and infinitely sharp. It pierces and separates the soul and spirit, bringing to light every thought, desire, and intent of the heart. It separates that which is of the Spirit from that of the flesh. Everyone and everything is made manifest by the Word of God. Every vestige of the clothing of flesh is consumed, leaving all who pass through this sword naked, open wide, and alive in Christ.

The imaginative mind will take the written word and create apparitions to make things appear as though they are real. A flaming sword in the hands of the cherubim speaks clearly of the same deception. In Genesis 3:24, "flaming" is translated from the Hebrew word *lahat*.[32] But *lahat* also appears in Exodus 7:11, where it is translated as "enchantments." "Then Pharaoh also called the wise men and the sorcerer's: now the magicians of Egypt, they also did in like manner with their enchantments [*lahat*]." *Strong's Concordance* includes *incantations* in its definition of *lahat*.

In defining *cherub*, *Strong's Concordance* also makes reference to droughts, cutting instruments, and desolating, destroying, killing, and slaying.[33] The sword can symbolize the Word of God, but we need to understand that a sword is a weapon of war and the word of the sword brings war and destruction. In Matthew 10:34, Jesus says, "Think not that I am come to send peace on earth: I came not to send peace, but a sword."

Jesus is the prince of peace and the sword is not the only word He brings. Regardless of who holds the sword, it brings devastation, famine, and destruction. The letter of the word kills and destroys all upon whom it falls. It brings drought to souls it pierces, cuts and slashes, and it leaves its victims hurting and bleeding. The sword has two edges—it cuts both the person who holds it and the person against whom it is used. It measures back to the one who lives by the sword, heaped up, pressed down, and running over. Whether the word is living or dead, it will minister the same life or death to its speaker. As we read in Proverbs 18:20–21, "A man's belly

---

[32] *Strong's Concordance* 3858.
[33] *Strong's Concordance* 2719, 32717

shall be satisfied with the fruit of his mouth; and with the increase of his lips shall he be filled. Death and life are in the tongue: and they that live it shall eat the fruit thereof."

In Revelation 13:10, John says this about the letter of the word (sword): "He that leadeth into captivity shall go into captivity: he that killeth with the sword [word] must be killed with the sword [word]. Here is the patience and the faith of the saints." Whether the fruit is life or death, the bearer of the sword and the victim both will eat of the same. The cherubim and the flaming sword bring death. They are faithful in guarding the Tree of Life, and its victims come to know a better way, Christ.

Cherubim

Exodus 25:18 says, "And thou shalt make two cherubim of gold; of beaten work shalt thou make them, in the two ends of the mercy seat." The cherubim are to guard the sacred things of God. They keep the way to the Tree of Life, to prevent man's entry into Eden, the garden of God. The cherubim can also be seen in the veil and curtains of the tabernacle. On the spiritual side of things, they are sewn into the letter of the law, also seen as man in the veil of his Adamic soul.

The Bible itself becomes a tool for the purpose of concealing God's mysteries. Most translations contain errors that serve to keep the hidden secrets from unworthy eyes, but even if the written word were pure, nothing would change. The interpretation of the scriptures, regardless of its accuracy, does not give us passage to life. Jesus Christ alone can do that.

For man to have life, he must get to the Tree of Life, but there is a problem. He must first get past the cherubim and the flaming sword. Some believe that the Bible is no longer needed, since it is the letter that kills and thus has no place in their deep spiritual minds. But there is nothing wrong with the letter itself, for in the midst of it is the law, and the law is holy, as Paul says: "Therefore the law is holy, and the commandments holy, and just, and good" (Romans 7:12).

The problem lies in man trying to fulfill the law by the will and works of the flesh, which is impossible. The law is found in the center of God's most holy place, in the Ark of the Covenant. For it to be a holy thing to us, we need to know it from this dimension—from within, rather than from without. As Romans 8:3–4 says, "For what the law could not do, in that it was weak through the flesh, God sending His own son in the likeness of sinful flesh, and for sin, condemned sin in the flesh: That the righteousness of the law might be fulfilled in us, who walk not after the flesh, but after the Spirit." The law itself is not wrong. The problem is in how the law is perceived, whether it is from within or without. The law was given not to save man, but to show how we need a savior.

"So he drove out the man; and placed at the east of the Garden of Eden Cherubim and a flaming sword which turned every way, to keep the way of the tree of life" (Genesis 3:24). The English word *keep* is a translation of the Hebrew word *shamar*, which means "root, to hedge about, to guard, to protect, and attend to."[34] This speaks of God's determination to keep man of the earth out of the garden, and it reveals what great care He placed over it. The cherubim over the mercy seat of the ark are in the image of God, but not as fallen men covered with dust; instead, they are conformed men and made of pure gold. The cherubim are holy, but not carnal men.

God would not allow the cherubim, the imaginings and thoughts of man, into the Holy of Holies, the paradise of God. These cherubim are contained or woven into the fiber of the veil and the curtains. The cherubim over the mercy seat are of the higher order. Men with lower imaginations are not allowed a place on His throne. Only those in Christ have that honor.

What Is the Difference in These Two Cherubim?

"And thou shalt make a veil of blue, and purple, and scarlet, and fine twined linen of cunning work: with cherubim shall it be made" (Exodus 26:31). The cherubim of the veil are of cunning work, but the cherubim of the mercy seat are of gold, a beaten work by man's hand. The veil represents self and speaks of the flesh. The souls within the cherubim are cunningly

---

[34] *Strong's Concordance* 8104.

woven. In the very fabric of man's thinking and imagination, the cherubim are the inseparable part of man.

Cherubims are made from the earthy materials with spiritual potentials to change.

In Exodus 26:31, the Hebrew word for "cunning" is *chashab*, meaning "to plait or weave; to fabricate, plot, or contrive; to think, regard, value, or compute."[35] This "cunning" work sounds like the work of the soul, and it is here where the cherubim are woven into the fabric of man's thinking. The very nature and works of the human soul, at their best, are a cunning fabrication of human thinking.

The cherubim of the mercy seat are not a cunning work, but a work that forms God's nature into heavenly creatures. They have substance that God can express Himself. How? Romans 12:2 tells us, "And be not conformed to this world: but be ye transformed by the renewing of your mind, that ye may prove what is that good, and acceptable, and perfect, will of God." The cherubim of the mercy seat are transformed. God's mind is in their mind. The cherubim and the mercy seat are of one substance, which is God.

"And he made the mercy seat of pure gold: two cubits and a half was the length thereof, and one cubit and a half the breadth thereof. And he made two cherubim of gold, beaten out of one piece made he them, on the two ends of the mercy seat" (Exodus 37:6–7). Again, the mercy seat and the cherubim are of one substance, gold hammered into one piece.

If we recall that cherubim, according to *Strong's Concordance*, are "imagination" and "thoughts," these become beaten together into one, changed and transformed into pure gold. When our imagination and thoughts rise to the mercy seat and turn to gold, we pass the veil of flesh because the cherubim (imagination and thoughts) have been changed by the renewing of the mind. God's mind becomes our mind, His will becomes our will, His purpose becomes our purpose, His thoughts become our thoughts, and His Spirit becomes our spirit. The cherubim and the mercy seat become one.

---

[35] *Strong's Concordance* 2803.

How Do God and Man Become One?

Let us go through the steps needed to become one, as in a marriage:

1. "Let this mind be in you, which was also in Christ Jesus: Who, being in the form of God, thought it not robbery to be equal with God" (Philippians 2:5–6).
2. "And when the day of Pentecost was fully come, they were all with one accord in one place" (Acts 2:1).
3. "I beseech Euodias, and beseech Syntyche, that they be of the same mind in the Lord" (Philippians 4:2).
4. "For this is the covenant that I will make with the house of Israel after those days, saith the Lord; I will put my laws into their mind, and I will be to them a God, and they shall be to me a people" (Hebrews 8:10).
5. "But he that is joined unto the Lord is one spirit" (1 Corinthians 6:17).

We found five things that will join man to God. When all are fused together, we are joined together into one spirit, which is Christ and you. When you become one of His, He will put His law in your mind and heart. The law that was in the ark made of stone is now in the Ark of the Covenant within you, and Christ is the lid that sits on the mercy seat. The oneness of man and Christ manifests the acceptable and perfect will of God as one.

The Lord Jesus Christ sits on the top of the ark—on the lid, the mercy seat—and under Him is the law secured. The cherubim have raised wings and face each other, with their eyes on the lid, the mercy seat, which is Christ. The cherubim (imagination, thoughts) that are in our minds should also be looking down toward the mercy seat and Christ, and always raising our wings (arms) above our heads and giving praise to Him.

Genesis 1:26 says, "And God said, let us make man in our image, after our likeness." This is what God was thinking. In His likeness, and from His own thoughts and imaginations, came a cherub. God is a spirit, and He took His spirit and made a viable man of the earth, with a choice to be separated or to become equal in God's image and likeness.

The golden cherubim over the mercy seat are creations directly from God, imaginings that are patterned after the character of God's Christ. The cherubim that are woven into the veil and curtains are man's fleshly mind. The thoughts of God are gold, and they are made manifest into sons.

The first Adam failed, because the imagination (cherubim) in Adam caused him to become unfit for his position in the eyes of God. The second Adam was also a covering cherub like the first man, Adam. The second Adam keeps the sanctuaries clean and undefiled, making a way back to Eden. The word *cherub* was also the name of a city, which means "blessing."[36] The English language always uses *cherubim* to refer to angels, but that is not the case with Greek and Hebrew. The city Cherub is mentioned in Ezra 2:59. We need to remember that the Bible was written in Hebrew, not English. And since Hebrew is the foundation of our knowledge of the Bible, we should stay as close as possible to the Hebrew meanings of words found in the Bible.

Many people have been taught that the cherubim that appear in Ezekiel are related to the story of the fall of Satan. There is nothing to suggest that this cherub was Satan, although that has often been assumed to be true. Ezekiel 1:3 strongly suggests that someone besides Ezekiel wrote and recorded the event. The scripture could be about Adam, who became a Satan (adversary) to God because he and Eve sinned by disobeying God. The story in Ezekiel is about someone breaking the command of God. In Adam's case, it was his unrighteousness that got him in trouble. Adam was a cherub, a protector. He was supposed to keep the garden and till it.

In our studies, we have seen that *Satan* is only a Hebrew word, not a real person that means to attack or accuse, to be an adversary or resist.[37] *Strong's* also defines the word *Satan* as an opponent, the archenemy of good, and an adversary.[38] The adversary of God could be anyone who opposes what God desires—in other words, a sinner. Anyone who is less than obedient and righteousness is a "Satan" to God, by definition. Satan is the character and behavior of a sinful person who hinders the work of God in any way. Satan is not a fallen angel, but a fallen man who was once

---

[36] *Strong's Concordance* 3742.

[37] *Strong's Concordance* H7853.

[38] *Strong's Concordance* H7854.

an anointed cherub in the garden of God—the heart of God from which man came, called Adam, the cherub of God.

To be in the heart of God is to be in God's garden, in God's mind and imagination. He created man in His image (likeness), as a cherub-man. Before anything can come into existence, it must first be imagined. Matthew 12:34 says that "out of the abundance of the heart, the mouth speaketh." Likewise, out of the mouth (heart) of God came man. "And God said; Let us make man in our image, after our likeness: So God created man in his image." (Genesis 1:26–27). Like Father, like son. If you see one, you see the other—the same spirit and character in each.

When God created him, Adam was in God's image and likeness, until he fell. Adam was the cherub or blessing that God created outside the garden, and God brought Adam into the garden with a job to do. "And the Lord God took the man, and put him into the Garden of Eden to dress it and to keep it" (Genesis 2:15).

The first Adam that God placed in the garden fell, and God was not pleased with the cherub that He had created (imagined). The cherubim that follow the first Adam will always fail, because they are fleshly, weak, and carnal. When Adam fell, he lost the image and the likeness of his creator. Adam sinned, which disqualified him and caused him to lose his position in the garden of God.

The reason for Adam's failure was that his mind-set (cherubim) was woven into the veil and curtain-flesh. He lost paradise, his light in the world. Adam was uncovered, naked and ashamed, and he needed a covering. So God gave him a coat of skin to wear until a better covering was available. Adam had his chance to be the king, with dominion over everything, but his mind (cherubim) was fleshly and not spiritual.

Adam would have returned to the garden, but God prevented it. We must remember that there is a word that is fleshly (cherubim, imagination), and there is a word that is spiritual. One is the letter of the word that kills, and the other is the word that quickens and gives life. The cherubim of gold are imaginings that are pure and like God.

Those of the letter of the word cannot find the way back to Eden, the garden of God. The cherubim God set at the east of the garden protect the gate and the way. For man to find the way, his cherubim cannot be of the woven veil of the curtain. His cherubim must be of the golden altar where God and man are in agreement.

People who have not become one with God cannot see, hear, or understand how to find the way into the Garden of Eden. The Word of God is protected, as we read in John 5:39: "Search the scriptures; for in them ye think ye have eternal life: and they are they which testify of me." Only a few people will find the way and enter therein. The Word of God is clear about who will understand and who will not.

Second Timothy 3:16 says, "All scriptures are given by inspiration of God." God reveals His Word by inspiration and through people who testify about Him. The cherubim (mind) of someone who is of the woven veil cannot know the way. "And they understood none of these things: and this saying was hid from them, neither knew they the things which were spoken" (Luke 18:34). They couldn't understand because they were spiritually blind. But when a person enters the garden, he becomes a son.

——— The Cherubim of the Natural Man ———

Let's look again at the meaning of *cherubim*. The root word in Hebrew is *keruwg*, meaning "to cut as with an ax, knife, sword, dagger, sword, mattock, or other tool." Anyone who tries to pass this cherub will be faced with the flaming sword that will cut them asunder. The cherub or *keruwg* is to "keep" the way of "tselem," the root word of which means "a shade, a phantom, an illusion, a representative figure, image, or vain show."[39] We see a cherub as a tool, not as an angel to keep man from the Garden of Eden, to keep the image (*tselem*) of God as a shade or imagination.

"But the natural man receiveth not the things of the Spirit of God; for they are foolishness unto him; neither can he know them, because they are spiritually discerned" (1 Corinthians 2:14). The carnal mind of the flesh cannot understand. Understanding is for those who are in Christ spiritually. "But as it is written, Eye hath not seen, not ear heard, neither have entered into the heart of man, the things which God hath prepared for them that love him. But God hath revealed them unto us by

---

[39] *Strong's Concordance* 6754.

his Spirit; for the Spirit searcheth all things, yea, the deep things of God" (1 Corinthians 2:9–10).

Why Cannot the Natural Man See the Deep Things of God?

The natural man cannot find his way back into the Garden of Eden, because he cannot find the key or the way to the Tree of Life. "And to make all men see what is the fellowship of the mystery, which from the beginning of the world hath been hid in God" (Ephesians 3:9). God hid His mystery from the world, like He hid the body of Moses, never to be found. The mysteries of God are revealed only to His saints. As Colossians 1:26 says, "Even the mystery which hath been hid from ages and from generations, but now is made manifest to His saints." The man to whom God would make known the riches of the spirit has hid himself inside the temple of God. Carnal man cannot see or hear him until he finds a way past the flaming sword of the cherubim that protects and keeps the way to the Tree of Life in the garden.

Man is dust of the earth, after the image of Adam, which must die or be killed. The flesh, the carnal mind, all must be changed. To enter the garden, one must die.

What Must Be Changed?

In 2 Corinthians, we learn how to gain entry to the Garden of Eden and the Tree of Life. "For the weapons of our warfare are not carnal, but mighty through God to the pulling down of strongholds. Casting down imaginations, and every high thing that exalteth itself against the knowledge of God, and bringing into captivity every thought to the obedience of Christ" (2 Corinthians 10:4–5). There it is.

The Bible is the letter of God to man, and it is written in a way to shade or shadow the things to come. It hides the way to the Tree of Life from carnal and fleshly minds. Cherubim hide the meaning of the way by not permitting the natural man to understand the mysteries of God. The people who can see are those who have been cut to pieces and beaten into one piece of gold, as on the lid of the mercy seat—one solid piece of the same material. It is only through Christ that the stone is removed from the Word of God, whereas the letter of the word kills. The purpose of the cherubim is to protect the holiness of God from the carnal.

———— Man in God's Image? How? ————

Man was created by God. God gave him a body, a soul, and His spirit—which together make up the temple of God in man, where God can come and present Himself. God is seated deep within man's heart and emotions. To understand this, we need to study the story of the tabernacle, its departments, and how it was laid out.

The most holy place was hidden where man couldn't see it. Nor could man even approach it until he went through the gate past the altar of incense, which is in the tabernacle's most holy place. God dwells in the holy place, where He talks to people who have cleansed themselves and are counted worthy to enter His glory and shine as a candle.

The mercy seat, where God sits, is in the place of His greatest glory—behind the curtain in the Holies of Holies, where nothing unclean enters. The curtain represents man's makeup—his flesh, soul, mind, will, intellect, and emotion. Cherubim were woven into the curtain to give a sense of God's glory. But here we find flesh in the fabric, the lust of the eye, the flesh, and the pride of life. This is dust—man woven into the fabric of the curtain. The curtain also functions as a filter, stopping dust and unclean things from coming through, and it makes people think that what they're seeing is only a shadow.

Paul said, "And over it the cherubim of glory shadowing the mercy seat of which we cannot now speak particularly" (Hebrews 9:5). These cherubim cover and overshadow the mercy seat, concealing the Lord with their eyes fixed on Him. These sons of God are in the image of God and keep this holy place secure. This is the place where God meets man in His glory. "And there I will meet with thee, and I will commune with thee from above the mercy seat, from between the two cherubim which are upon the ark of the testimony" (Exodus 25:22).

The Strong's Greek word for "overshadow" is *kataskiazo* meaning "to overshade or cast a shade upon."[40] The cherubim cover, protect, and guard the mercy seat just as the cherubim with the flaming sword that kept Adam from returning to the garden.

Christ is the exact image of God. When you see Christ, you see God's glory, but hidden in the fleshly body of Christ. From the birth of Christ to His death, and despite all the miracles He performed, most people couldn't see His greater glory. The only exception was a man named Simeon. Only when people's eyes were opened could they see and understand that Jesus was the Christ, the Son of the living God, born from above.

Jesus was killed on a cross and His body was placed in a tomb. Three days later, He was raised by the Spirit of God. Then He was seen by, and talked to, many people who witnessed Him being alive. He told people to go to Jerusalem and tarry until they received power from on high. Finally, as described in Acts.1:9, "And when he had spoken these things, while they beheld, he was taken up; and a cloud received him out of their sight."

We need to pay attention to this cloud that took Jesus from the earth out of sight. He ascended in a cloud into heaven, and He returned in a cloud on the day of Pentecost, when thousands of souls were saved.

—— How Do We Know He Has Returned? ——

"Ye men of Galilee, why stand ye gazing up into heaven? This same Jesus, which is taken up from you into heaven, shall so come in like manner as ye have seen Him go into heaven" (Acts 1:11). The great cloud that received Jesus on the day of Pentecost was in the upper room, and that cloud has been growing larger every day since then.

The clouds represent God's people, and the Word said Jesus would return from heaven in a cloud—not as a physical body, but in spirit and great power. Psalms 68:34 says, "Ascribe ye strength unto God: his Excellency is over Israel, and his strength is in the clouds." Those clouds contain the saints of God, who is in heaven, whether here or in the clouds.

---

[40] Strong's Greek Concordance G2683 from G2596 (*kata*) and G4639 (*akia*) darkness, shadow, covers.

In Ephesians 2:6, we read that God "hath raised us up together, and made us sit together in heavenly places in Christ Jesus." Those who have Christ in their temple have already been raised up (rapture) to sit together in heavenly places in the spirit. The clouds in heaven are the believers, and when Jesus left us, He promised that He would return in clouds with His saints.

The glory of God is seen only in part, as if we are looking through a glass. The fullness of God's glory is not seen; however, we do see God through Christ in man. We will one day see Him as He is. We cannot see God's face until we become transformed by His Spirit. God protects man from seeing Him as He is, because doing so would cause many to die. The cherubim protect the way, but they are seen only through the curtain as they overshadow the mercy seat in the holy of holies.

Since Adam was cast out of Eden and the cherub began protecting the way, people have tried to find another way to the Tree of Life. But Jesus has told us, "Verily, verily, I say unto you, He that entereth not by the door into the sheepfold, but climbeth up some other way, the same is a thief and a robber" (John 10:1). Jesus knew that people didn't like the thought of facing the flaming sword of the cherubim that protected the way to the Tree of Life. Man does not like the idea of dying by the sword. Flesh must die before we can enter the garden of God.

The temple of God is inside us and placed deep in the heart where the mercy seat sits, and so does God. "Know ye not that ye are the temple of God, and that the Spirit of God dwelleth in you? If any man defile the temple of God, him shall God destroy; for the temple of God is holy, which temple ye are" (1 Corinthians 3:16–17). We are the temple where God's glory should live, like a cloud full of thunder and lightning. But many people have lost that thunderous cloud and the glory that fills the house of God. The temple inside man where God sits has changed over time.

If the cherubim (our imaginings or thoughts) are not looking toward the mercy seat where God sits, then they are woven into the curtain. And we become like Solomon's temple, void of a mercy seat and a covering of cherubim. Those things are removed, leaving us with only the ark and the tablets of stone. God covers His glory with a cloud.

Ezekiel saw the cloud of God's glory in the cherub, and it was a bright cloud. "Then the glory of the Lord went up from the cherub, and stood over the threshold of the house; and the house was filled with the cloud, and the court was full of the brightness of the Lord's glory" (Ezekiel 10:4).

There was a different scene at Solomon's temple—no bright cloud, but only a dark cloud. "And it came to pass, when the priests were come out of the holy place, that the cloud filled the house of the Lord, so that the priests could not stand to minister because of the cloud: for the glory of the Lord had filled the house of the Lord. Then spake Solomon, the Lord said that he would dwell in the thick darkness" (1 Kings 8:10–12). This is true today, that God is hidden in the thick darkness, invisible to man.

Churches today build houses to God and fill them up with tradition and things of the world. The holiness of God's glory is not seen there, only the greatness of the churches and what we have done to please ourselves. Our churches have become, like Babylon, places of confusion.

Where There Is No Ark

We need always to behold the ark of God, so that we may comfort one another in hope. In these verses, the women could well represent the church of today. "And about the time of her death the women that stood by her said unto her, Fear not; for thou hast borne a son. But she answered not, neither did she regard it. And she named the child Ichabod, saying, the glory is departed from Israel: because the ark of God was taken, and because of her father in law and her husband. And she said the glory is departed from Israel: for the ark of God is taken" (1 Samuel 4:20–22).

When the ark is removed, no glory is present. We must move on toward Eden, the garden of God, and not let the problems we face each day stop us. Once you taste the holiness of God and see His cloud of glory, don't stop. We have not yet seen the fullness of God's glory, because we need to pass the flaming sword of the cherubim at the east side of Eden.

Christ sits on the mercy seat in the temple, and the sons of God are happy to fellowship with one person or a house full of people. Sons of God do not need great buildings to show the glory of God in the clouds. We do not need to have ourselves recognized. The self is dead and the flesh is crucified in Christ. Only the glory can be seen, because we have been transformed into gold by the renewing of our minds.

When the cherubim (the imaginings of the mind) are one in Christ, and when their spirit is raised to a higher level in God, so also the wheels (thoughts) are lifted up. They rise together and God is visible at the top of the cherubim in our heads.

Circle of Life

"I am Alpha and Omega, the beginning and the ending, saith the Lord, which is, and which was, and which is to come, the Almighty" (Revelation 1:8). The Lord is both the starting point and the ending point, where all things start and return. God is like a ring in which all points come together and form a circle. This is true in all things. Out of dust came man, and man will return to dust. We read in Genesis 2:7 that "And the God formed man of the dust of the ground." And again in Genesis 3:19, "In the sweat of thy face shalt thou eat bread, till thou return unto the ground; for out of it wast thou taken: for dust thou art, and unto dust shalt thou return." This is the body, the flesh that will return to the ground, not the spirit of man. The spirit in man is a part of God, who gave the body life. Everything returns to the source from which it was created—body to earth, spirit to God.

"Then shall the dust return to the earth as it was: and the spirit shall return unto God who gave it" (Ecclesiastes 12:7). God has given man a spirit that rest in the minds, thoughts, and imagination (the cherubim). Everything is the Lord's, and He distributes it as He see fit.

Ezekiel's Cherubim

There are many interpretations of Ezekiel's vision. In Ezekiel 28:14, we find cherubim just as the one at the gate to the Garden of Eden. Cherubim are tools of God, to use as He needs to protect His interest. What Ezekiel saw while in the Spirit looked real—just like the cherubim with the flaming sword who stood at the gate to the garden? Ezekiel is looking also at another cherub:

> Thou hast been in Eden [Adam] the garden of God; every
> precious stone was thy covering, the sardius, topaz, and

the diamond, the beryl, the onyx, and the jasper, the sapphire, the emerald, and the carbuncle, and gold: the workmanship of the tabrets and of the pipes was prepared in thee in the day that thou wast created. Thou art the anointed cherub that covereth; and I have set thee so: thou wast upon the holy mountain of God; thou hast walked up and down in the midst of the stones of fire. Thou wast perfect in thy ways from the day that thou wast created, till iniquity was found in thee. By the multitude of thy merchandise they have filled the midst of thee with violence, and thou hast sinned: therefore I will cast thee as profane out of the mountain of God: and I will destroy thee, O covering cherub, from the midst of the stones of fire. Thine heart was lifted up because of thy beauty, thou hast corrupted thy wisdom by reason of thy brightness, I will cast thee before kings, that they may behold thee. Thou hast defiled thy sanctuaries by the multitude of thine iniquities, by the iniquity of thy traffic; therefore will I bring forth a fire from the midst of thee, it shall devour thee, and I will bring thee to ashes upon the earth in the sight of all them that behold thee. (Ezekiel 28:13–18)

Adam was a cherub in the day he was created perfect and he was in the mountain of God, or the kingdom and paradise of God. The day he sinned, he lost his position in the kingdom or paradise of God and was cast down. Adam became one of the cherubim of the veil.

We must not forget that man is the temple of God, the sanctuary where God talks to man. In man there are the cherubim that are woven into our minds, and the cherubim that sit deep in our hearts and emotions. Where a man goes, so go the cherubim. Adam lost his brightness when he disobeyed the Lord, and man lost his candlelight and was darkened.

The cherub that covereth is when man lives, in the holiness of God with pure and clean thoughts. Otherwise it's the cherub of the curtain that blocks us from the glory of God that lives *beyond* the curtain. And none of this involves Satan or a supernatural angel that fell from heaven, as some believe.

Man needs to hear the call of God in the temple. This temple—the body—is the house of God. Hebrews 3:6 says, "But Christ as a son over his own house [body]; whose house are we." In the house, the body, the temple of God is in man, as Ezekiel said: "Then the glory of the Lord went up from the cherub, and stood over the threshold of the house; and the house was filled with the cloud, and the court was full of the brightness of the Lord's glory" (Ezekiel 10:4).

The sound of the cherubim's wings was heard in the outer court, as God spoke. When is the last time you, as a cherub, entered into the Holy of Holies, where God can speak and cover you with His glory, or cause you to stand in the doorway of the house, raise your wings, and clap your hands so that it can be heard outside of the house? When the inside of the house is filled with the Spirit of God, it will be heard outside in the courtyard.

When Ezekiel saw and heard the wings as the voice of God, he was referring to what it took to lift up the God of creation. Those who live in the cloud and share the glory of God will always hear thunder and lightning within themselves. Every time one of His sons hears the voice of God, there will be thunder.

The wings speak of what it takes to be lifted up and fly. The wings and the voice of God are one and the same. The two cherubim represent the minds of the sons and the mind of Christ, beaten out of pure gold, of one mind, and coming from the Word of God. The glory of God is visible in man when he becomes of one mind with Christ.

Paul tells the church at Philippi, "Let this mind be in you, which was also in Christ Jesus" (Philippians 2:5). In the house (sanctuary), the temple of God is in man. When his thoughts, and imagination (cherubim) raises. Then the house will be filled with the glory of God.

Man is about to end his trip in the flesh, and a change is going to take place. God's Word will go into all corners of the earth [Body]. The Spirit of God and His sons are all one, and the mind of God and the mind of the sons are one. When all the wheels move together—the spirit, body, and soul—then man in God and God in man move together, including the cherubim.

It is God who sits on the cherub and controls the wings, the wheels, and the four heads. When God rises, everything rises with him, by this spirit or power. Ezekiel saw living creatures by the river *Chebar*, a Hebrew word that can be defined as "extent of time, a great while, hence long ago, formerly, hitherto, already, or now."[41] *Kabar* means "to plait together, to augment in number or quality, to accumulate in abundance or multiply."[42]

The Hebrew word for "river" is *nahar*, which means "to sparkle, be cheerful, hence from the sheen of a running stream, to flow, assemble, to flow together, be lighted."[43] *Nehar* means "a river or stream," such as the Euphrates, symbolizing prosperity.[44]

According to the original Hebrew, Ezekiel could see from the east of Eden to the river of Chebar, which symbolizes an extended length of time, a flow of time from long ago to this day. This river flowed beside the garden of God and had four heads, in the Genesis account. It flowed in all directions, from the center of the garden, and watered the earth. Since Adam fell, the river is still running but not as clearly as it once did. When it flows closer to Jesus Christ, the river is clean and good to drink, because it flows from the throne of God (see Revelation 22:1–20).

The cherubim can be your best friend or your worst enemy. They can lift you up into the glory of God or destroy you in the fires of God's wrath. The Lord has sent His cherubim out to mark all of God's people, and at the end of the day, those who have the mark applied to their foreheads will die. We must rebuke evil in all forms and drink daily from the river of Chebar, the river of life, and the blood of Christ. His glory and power will be revealed and all flesh shall see it. "And the glory of the Lord shall be revealed, and all flesh shall see it together: for the mouth of the Lord hath spoken it" (Isaiah 40:5).

The cherubim (thoughts) that are within you will be judged by God. Every cherub will stand and give an account of every thought and idle word (see Matthew 12:36). The cherub within you is the devil that must be dealt with and destroyed, so that you can be raised up in Christ as a new creature, a new man, and a new Adam. God will cast out Satan from heaven (your mind) and destroy him, and he will never be remembered.

Cherubim can be good or evil. Some say that Satan was a cherub

---

41 *Strong's Concordance* 3528. (Also see *kebar*.)

42 *Strong's Concordance* 3527.

43 *Strong's Concordance* H5102.

44 *Strong's Concordance* H5104.

who fell, did evil, and became the devil of today. If that's true, then what is keeping us from entering the garden of God, a supernatural fallen angel? The Bible contains no evidence or proof that a devil from heaven is the problem. It is the cherubim within a person that is the problem. The cherubim within must destroy all strongholds and evil thoughts and imaginations that are opposed to God. What are they? What defiles a man?

In Matthew 15:18–20, we read, "But those things which proceed out of the mouth come forth from the heart [mind, thoughts, and desires], and they defile the man. Out of the heart proceeds evil thoughts, murder, adulteries, fornications, thefts, false witness, blasphemes. These are the things which defile a man." These things are the devils within that need to be killed by the renewing of the mind. Not by confession, but by changing direction. Confession is not repentance. Changing direction and turning your life around is repentance.

Helps

Hebrew and Greek Words with Definitions

1. Cherub   (KHAW-RAB) Hebrew: the prime root means to parch through drought, destroy, kill, slay, lay waste. (*Strong's Concordance* 2717)

1a. Cherub   (KHARAB) Hebrew/Chaldean: to demolish, destroy. (*Strong's Concordance* 2718)

1b. Chereb   (KHEH'-REB) Hebrew: a cutting instrument, knife, sword, sharp implement, axe, dagger, and mattock. (*Strong's Concordance* 2718)

1c. Chareb   (KHAW-RABE) Hebrew: to parch, ruin, desolate, dry, waste. (*Strong's Concordance* 2720)

2. Angel   (MALAK) Hebrew: to dispatch as a deputy, prophet, priest, teacher, ambassador, angel, king. (*Strong's Concordance* 4397)

2a. Angel   (MEL-AW-KAW) Hebrew: deputyship, ministry, employ, mentor, work. (*Strong's Concordance*, the same as 4399)

3. Keruwb   (KER-OOB) A cherub, imaginary figure. Same as 3743. Kerub: a city in Babylon. (*Strong's Concordance* 3742)

4. Image   (TSELEM) Root means to shade, a phantom, illusion, resemblance, representation figure, image, vain shew. (*Strong's Concordance* 6754)

4a. Image   (TSELEM) Chaldean/Hebrew: form, image. (*Strong's Concordance* H6755)

5. Flaming   (LAHAT) a blaze, magic flaming, enchantment. (*Strong's Concordance* 3858) Also burn up, set on fire, flaming, kindle. (*Strong's Concordance* 3857)

Special note: If a cherub is an angel of God, why does he have wheels under him and why does God ride on his back with a seat upon him? "And he rode upon a cherub, and did fly: and he was seen upon the wings of the wind" (2 Samuel 22:11). Wind is invisible and cannot be seen with the natural eye, neither can one see the thoughts of a man. Yet both are real and can have good and bad effects on one's life. Wings of a person's mind are the thoughts that move quickly as lighting in the head [heaven] which can have effects on earth.[the body]

Helps

Hebrew and Greek Words and Theme Meaning

6. Keep   (SHAMAR) Hebrew: to hedge about, guard, protect, attend to, beware, take heed to self, keep mark, look narrowly, observe, preserve, reserve, save self, wait for, watchman. (*Strong's Concordance* 8104)

7. Woven   (CHASHAB) to plait or interpenetrate, weave, fabricate, plot or contrive, think, regard, valve, compute, devise, esteem, find out, forecast, hold, imagine, invent, be like. (*Strong's Concordance* 2803; same as 2804)

8. Satan   (SAW-TAN) to attack, accuse, be an adversary, resist. Note: there is no falling supernatural angel mentioned in this reference. (*Strong's Concordance* 7853)

8a. Satan   (SAW-TAWN) an opponent, the archenemy of good, adversary, Satan, withstand. Note: this refers to anyone or anybody that acts against the will of God. (*Strong's Concordance* 7854)

9. Overshadow   (KATASKIAZO, KATA, and SKIA) Greek: to shade, a shadow, darkness of error, cover. (*Strong's Concordance* G2683, G2596, G4639)

10. Chevar   (KABAR) to augment quality, accumulate in abundance, multiply. (*Strong's Concordance* 3527)

11. Cheber   (KEGAR) Extent of time, a great while, hence long ago, already. (*Strong's Concordance* 3528)

12. River   (NAHAR) Hebrew. (*Strong's Concordance* 5104)

12a. River   (GICHON) Hebrew: a stream, a river. (*Strong's Concordance* 1518)

References

Cruden, Alexander. *Cruden's Complete Concordance.* Zondervan Publishing House, 1967

The Companion Bible: E.W. Bullinger, Kregel Publishers Grand Rapids, MI 1922.

Erman, Adolf. *Life in Ancient Egypt.* English Translation. London, New York, Macmillan & Co. Translated, by H.M. Tiard, 1894 page 282. Also the

History of the Devil, Carus, Paul, Kindle Edition, Evinity Publishing Inc. 2009, Page 15-17.

Hastings, James. *Encyclopedia of Religion and Ethics,* vol.4. Page 578-579, T & T Publishers, Edinburgh. 1908-1926

Harpers Bible Dictionary: HarperCollins Publishers, New York N.Y. 1985 Page 582.

Jobes, Gertrude. *Dictionary of Mythology Folklore and Symbols.* New York: Scarecrow, 1961.

King James Bible. 1611. Nashville, TN: Thomas Nelson, 1976.

King James Bible: Authorized Version. Frank Charles Thompson, ed. 1909. Indianapolis, IN: B.B. Kirkbride Bible Co., 1964.

Liddell and Scott. *Greek-English Lexicon.* Oxford University Press, Oxford 1871, 1987

The Interpreters Dictionary of the Bible: Buttrick, A. George, Abingdon Press, 1962 16th Ed.

The Life Application Bible. Tyndale House. Iowa Falls, IA: World Bible Publishers, 1988.

Odell, M. E. "Preparing the Way." *The New Library of Catholic Knowledge,* Volume 1. N.P.: Hawthorn Books, 1963.Page 2

Pritchard, James B., ed. *Ancient* Near *Eastern Texts Relating to the Old Testament.* Princeton: Princeton UP. 1969 *An Egyptian Letter,* Wilson, A. John page 475-477.

Laurence, Richard. *The Book of Enoch*,1883. R.H. Charles, 1917 Publisher.

Stern, David H. *Complete Jewish Bible: An English Version of the Tanakh (Old Testament) and B'Rit Hadashah (New Testament)*. N.P.: Messianic Jewish Publications, 1998. Clarksville, MD

Strong, James. *Strong's Exhaustive Concordance of the Bible*. 1890. Madison, NJ: Abingdon, 1986.

Test Questions

1. What did Jesus come to do on earth, other than save souls?
2. What did Jesus come to destroy in man? Explain your answer.
3. Define the "works" of the devil.
4. Define sin. How does the Bible define sin?
5. If Satan is the accuser of the brethren (Revelation 12:10), why is he not present at the great white throne judgment when Jesus is the mediator between God and man? Where is the accuser?
6. Who is the last enemy to be destroyed, and how? Explain.
7. In James 1:15, we read that "Sin bringeth forth Death." If sin is the cause of death, and death is the last enemy to be destroyed, which is the devil? Did Jesus destroy the devil by his death and resurrection? Explain. (See Hebrews 9:26 and 1 Peter 2:24.)
8. How does death come about? Is sin the cause? Explain. (1 John 3:8)
9. A war is going on between the flesh and spirit. Is flesh the accuser, or devil, that is warring against God? Explain.
10. In Romans 1:18, God does not come against a supernatural being—Satan, the devil—but against men who are ungodly and unrighteous. Explain why you do or do not believe in a personal Satan or devil. Indicate scripture that supports your claim.
11. Could God, the Creator, be a Satan or devil to someone? Satan means "adversary or accuser," and Proverbs 1:26 says, "I also will laugh at your calamity, I will mock when your fear cometh." Explain.
12. The Bible says that Satan, the devil, comes seeking to destroy and kill. "Be sober, be vigilant, because your adversary, [Satan] the devil, as a roaring lion, walketh about, seeking whom he may devour" (1 Peter 5:8). Who was this adversary? The devil that was seeking to destroy the saints in Peter's day was not supernatural, but the Roman government and its religion. Who were these individuals? Explain.

13. Jesus said that the adversary—Satan, the devil—lived in the church at Pergamum (Revelation 2:12). In John's day, Pergamum, known today as Turkey, was home to very rich worshippers of the Greek gods Zeus and Asclepius. Because of these gods, Antipas was killed. This throne seat is said to be in Germany today. Was any of this a supernatural being or just flesh-and-blood evil leaders of the empire? Explain.

14. "God spared not the angels that sinned, but cast them down to hell and delivered them into chains of darkness, to be reserved unto judgment" (2 Peter 2:4). Does the scripture say anywhere that angels were supposed to cause us any problems—to hurt us or tempt us to sin against God?

15. Verse 6 of Jude refers to "the angels that left their first estate." Does Jude say anything about activity intended to harm us or cause us to sin?

16. What about Satan in Isaiah 14:12–15 and Ezekiel 28:12–15? Don't these Bible passages prove Satan to be supernatural? Is there any scripture that says Satan is a heavenly being, or was Satan always earthbound?

17. In Numbers 22:22, the angel became an adversary. Was this holy angel a Satan to Balaam? Explain.

18. That which is in your heart will determine what you seek and desire to have, whether it is of the flesh or the spirit. Do you agree that we have individual choice? Explain your answer.

19. Jesus is our mediator, according to 1 Timothy 2:5. How? What is the responsibility of a mediator?

20. Write a 500-word report on your views about a supernatural adversary who was opposed to God and man.

21. Give a full detailed explanation of cherubim, providing references in your report to support your views.

Part Two: Cherubim

———— Test Questions ————

1. Does *Strong's Concordance* say that cherubim are angels?
2. Explain what a cherub is, according to *Strong's Concordance* and your Bible.
3. Did God send a cherub to stand and keep the way of the Tree of Life, or did He place a cherub? Explain what was placed there to protect the Tree of Life.
4. What was the purpose of the flaming sword, and what was it?
5. The garden of Eden was not to be destroyed, because the Tree of Life needed to be protected. Where is this garden today? Is it still protected by the cherubim?
6. The cherubim were told to protect the Tree of Life. What is this Tree of Life?
7. How were the cherubim told to keep the Tree of Life?
8. The flaming sword will burn and cut in all directions. What does this represent?
9. The English language did not exist at the time of the Hebrew writings on this subject. Can the English language be trusted on the subject? Explain.
10. Cherubim were handmade, true or false? Prove your answer.
11. Did God create man a cherub? Explain.
12. What will keep man from having access to the Tree of Life in the garden of God? Explain.

— Is Satan a Supernatural Fallen Angel? —

Revelation is a book going forward, not backward. What I am saying is based on what God the Creator and Father of Jesus said in the very beginning of the book. Everything that John said he heard happened while he was in the Spirit. God told Jesus to tell the angel to tell John that what he heard and saw would happen at a later date, shortly and hereafter (Revelation 1:1).

Regarding Satan, we know that he was not a supernatural angel cast from heaven, but a man who lived in the time of Job, Jesus, and John, and that he was an adversary or Satan toward the church.

Everything John saw was to be after his writing, sometimes later (Revelation 2:10 and 13). In the Jewish Bible, we read in chapter 1 of Revelation, "that must happen very soon." This is all about the adversary against the church, which would be ending very soon in his day.

Your comments and any response to this work are always welcome. This is a work for the purpose of a deeper study in the Word of God. This research is great for Bible students and teachers who can think outside of the box, when truth is really sought after.

Maston Love Jr., PhD

Made in the USA
Coppell, TX
29 October 2021

64856103R00100